A
BLACK
THREAD

JIMMI LOVE

DEDICATION

This book is dedicated first to my family. To those who are family through blood and those who are family through spirit. For my Jamaican, AmerIndian and Hebrew ancestors who came through struggle by strength, wit and tenacity whose voices have been silenced.

To the memory of my brother, James Davis
Murdered by Klansmen...

Also, for the youth who will someday lead. If you do not create your reality, you will find yourself living the reality of someone else.

CONTENTS

Acknowledgments   i

1   Points of View   1

2   Mysteries   8

3   Origins   20

4   The European Renaissance   37

5   The Revolutionary War   63

6   The Civil War   74

7   Hidden Colors   108

8   Unions   119

9   Natural Selection   131

10   Planned Parenthood of America   147

11   Domestic Terrorism   156

12   Sports   179

13   Civil Rights   198

14   Economic Sanctions   204

15   Music   230

16   Lost Data   246

Summary   255

ACKNOWLEDGMENTS

Thank you to all those who were insightful enough to have written the truth. Thank you to the leadership, all colors and races, who led, and lead with compassion and fairness.

CHAPTER 1

POINTS OF VIEW

"The definition of the word equality actually means "to be equal". It means to be the same."

1 POINTS OF VIEW

Spin

As with many fabrics, the quality is in the stitching. Friedrich Nietzsche wrote: *"Invisible threads are the strongest ties."* I say that when the thread is revealed, it can be followed to where that garment began...
So it is with the fabric of society. This book represents a collection of individual fibers that when spun together, produce a proper thread - *a black thread*. These elements may or may not share origins and therefore, may seem to be unrelated. A closer look reveals that these 'spun' fibers create threads that affect the very fabric of our collective existence. This book will show the individual fibers that make up this Black Thread and how it has, and in fact is, shaping all our lives.

Rewriting History

There seem to be many points of history that we have entrusted to 'scholars' or, those who have learned from others. One of the things that irritated me the most about Black history is that the renditions of that history were only accepted from White scholars who were initially taught by the Blacks from whom the history comes. In other words, Europeans have to validate my story in order for it to be accepted – even though I'm telling the same story, from a more reputable source and oftentimes, a first-hand perspective. The question is, can we blindly trust other opinions or perspective on the events that involve persons of color, which have occurred throughout time?

From the beginning, up through the 1940's, and even today in movies, in publications and books, Blacks have been portrayed in many a negative light. Blacks have been presented as lazy, buffoons, idiots and cowards with 'Stockholm Syndrome'. For example, in books like 'The Growth of the American Republic', written by professors Samuel E. Morrison and Henry Steele Commager, referring to the Blacks (or, as they call them 'Sambo'):

"As for Sambo, whose wrongs moved the Abolitionists to wrath and tears, there is some reason to believe that he suffered less than any other class in the South from its 'peculiar institution',".

The book goes on to say:

"Although brought to America by force, the incurably optimistic negro soon became attached to the country, and devoted to his 'white folks',".

Passages like these are the reason I had to include this section. As I've said many times before, "History is written by the masters or those who win the wars". What this means is that many significant occurrences and or achievements of those who were conquered or enslaved (such as Blacks in America), are often strategically eliminated from history as these, the victors see fit. In blaring contrast, the art and culture from these slaves and Blacks in general influenced

America's culture, and other cultures all around the world.

This dissemination of either fabricated or dismantled information clouds the truth. It instills pride in one race by dismantling another. If I have no heroes, what shall I emulate? The main problem I have with this is that it diminishes the 'I Can' in those young Black minds who may have the capacity to 'Do', as we humans emulate our heroes. For example, knowing things like George Washington Carver, the 'Plant-man', provided Henry Ford with the idea for mass production by looking at the Fibonacci sequence in nature (Thus, the facilities being called 'Plants'), lets me know that I too can make positive contributions to society.

Many live their lives in the hopes that their exploits and deeds inspire and influence others. With many of these accomplishments being overlooked or ignored, how can those of future generations emulate their hidden heroes? There has been a formula that has worked for millennia. This same modified formula "Destroy the religion and artifacts, and replace their culture" was written in the book 'The Grand Chessboard' written by Zbigniew Brzezinski in 1997.

In order for something to be a catalyst, it is logical to say that it first must have an impetus. Something about this place, person or thing had to give the initiator the idea to impact it, or them, in some way. In this case, what is it about people of color that would make entire regimes want to annihilate them? What about them would destroy their humanity so much, that killing them, their women and children would be just a thought? What type of mass insanity would have to grip a people so as to drive them to literally wipe out another people and their culture?

Creation of a Common Enemy

An enemy is defined as: "a person who is actively opposed or hostile to someone or something; someone who hates another; someone who attacks or tries to harm another; something that harms or threatens someone or something; a group of people (such as a nation) against whom another group is fighting a war". Here are some questions that many have asked for ages. Why would someone hate someone they've never met? How could someone whom one has never met become that person's enemy? What could make one entire group of people hate another entire group of people? Why would the accomplishments of a race be ignored or erased? It seems that it is in fact an organized agenda.

The powers that guide and control the projected outcomes of activity on this planet have for millennia used psychological warfare to divide and conquer its inhabitants. It has been, and is being done by creating financial inconsistency, ranking political hierarchy and drawing color lines. It is so easy to do when one has control over land, wealth, the media and media outlets. Recently, a young child of 8 asked me if I could EXPLAIN RACISM and this was my response:

"Imagine that GREEN aliens come to Earth. They have brought useful knowledge, influence international culture, and, are kind and loving. The issue is, whenever the aliens mate with humans, the result is a green human. At some point, if this were to continue, all humanoids would be green. In order to save our non-green species, we would have to either cease all interaction with the 'Greens' or take whatever measures necessary to stop the creation of green humans, or, eliminate these Greens all together. In this case, racism is the calculated and calibrated reaction to the fear of a 'Green' planet."

Hatred, fear and distrust in the guise of politics (or association) have been used for centuries to target and divide man. People usually band together against a common enemy - "The enemy of my friend is my enemy". All one has to do is to present the targeted group as a threat while presenting that group in contrast to another, preferred group.

Take for example, the Immigration Act of 1965 allowing Asians, Koreans and Slavics into America and calling them the 'model minorities'. They were given stipends and loans to purchase homes and start businesses and then, displayed as the success stories that many Blacks were not. Then, the narrative became "If they just got here, and they are prospering, why can't you?" This, more than anything else, is what drives criminal or nefarious activity, as it spawns a 'survival of the fittest' environment. Now, these 'criminals' and their crimes can be displayed as the reason for harsher treatment. One justification for the harsher treatment of these people is said to prevent them and their criminal activities from reaching mainstream society.

There are many ways to control populations and their governments, as well as their futures. 'Fear' is the most available, transferable, potent tool used to control the masses. All one has to do is announce the presence of the threat, describe it and then somehow, put it on display. The response is usually the congregation or banding together of those who feel threatened against their perceived enemy. This is evident in the creation of militia groups, as well as others who have assembled together against their common enemies.

The resurfacing of privatization proponent Right-winged groups such as The Heritage Foundation and the American Enterprise Institute represent this banding together. These independent, grassroots organizations and groups were also supported by representatives of the upper-crust, which included Joseph Coors, Richard Scaife, William E. Simon and others.

Many of these separatist groups use propaganda to sway the minds of their members and those whom they attract. These groups unite behind an icon or an ideal – each of which is clearly different and clearly visible i.e. a crest or flag, a political stance, a culture, a skin color and/or a cause. Some of these groups include: Missionary Merchants and Military; Ku Klux Klan; Nazi Party; The Liberty League; The American Firsters; The John Bircher Society; The McCarthyites; and The Tea Party. These groups were, or are, steeped in hatred and controversy as they pushed the Right agenda and inadvertently strengthened the political position of the top 1%.

The hatred of one culture to another is only one of the reasons for the dismantling of historical facts. The absence of the knowledge of one's self and origin of one's people weaken that individual. Even if that person's heredity is in question, the knowledge of one's ancestors is a powerful motivator.

While these situations, groups and incidences raise questions that beg for answers, there are other questions that seemingly have no answers – or at least, no clear answers.

one's people weaken that individual. Even if that person's heredity is in question, the knowledge of one's ancestors is a powerful motivator.

While these situations, groups and incidences raise questions that beg for answers, there are other questions that seemingly have no answers – or at least, no clear answers.

CHAPTER 2

MYSTERIES

"Were blacks the reason we now
have low or no-tolerance laws?
The evidence points to yes."

2 MYSTERIES

Unanswered Questions

It is said that philosophy is questions one cannot answer, and religion is answers we dare not question. So it seems with history and its philosophical questions about remnants of sites and activities from days gone by. So, people draw conclusions based again on the limits or expanse of individual knowledge or personal education. The more advanced the education, the more rigid or religious the stance.

Let's take the *Nasca Lines* for example. We are talking about the top of a mountain having been leveled or planed off apparently to facilitate flying machines – in a time when flying machines were said not to have existed. Who has the correct answer? Why does the obvious answer seem absurd? Why do we humans have the desire to distort things that can be clearly interpreted? Machu Picchu is another of these examples. We just come to conclusions based on our own individual degrees of education, abilities to interpret unknown facts or accept the ... interpretations of those before us i.e., Socrates, Copernicus, Galileo, Einstein and others. It is not unlike the successful prosecution of an innocent man based on circumstantial evidence. So, history is clouded with opinion and perspective in the guise of fact. Science involves the proving or disproving of unsubstantiated data through testing and trial and error. The issue here includes the methods of the testing and intensity of these methods.

Unexplained Civilizations

Where do we begin? Let's begin at what we have found to be the beginning. Many academics concur that the Homo line goes back at least 3 million years, and that 'modern' man evolved about a million years ago. The accepted timeline for Homo Sapien's migration across the planet is around 5000 years. However, with the discovery of a skull fragment during a Hungarian excavation, that theory is at least 600,000 years off. Hominid fossils of 1.77 million years old are unearthed in Dmmansi, Georgia and a hominid tooth dated 7 million years old was found in Miocene deposits near the Bulgarian Maritsa River. A seemingly contemporaneous environment in Australia yields remains of Neanderthal (stone-age), Homo erectus and Homo sapiens (modern-man). It was previously accepted that Homo erectus (1.55 million years) evolved from Homo habilis (1.44 million years). Fossils found in Kenya in 2007 reveal that Homo habilis and Homo çerectus lived side by side in Africa for at least 500,000 years.

More inconclusive evidence was found in Pershing County, Nevada in the form of a shoe print revealing fine double-stitched seams dating 400 million years ago. In America circa 1975, evidence of humans dating 40 million years ago were found in Oklahoma, Wisconsin and New Mexico where humanoid footprints were found by Dr. Stanley Rhine. In addition, Death Valley, much like the Sahara, was once a green paradise. The difference is that Death Valley was supposed to have been inhabited by a race of giants.

The fact that members of the fabled Zingh Empire reportedly sailed to the Americas more than 14,000 years ago means that they could very well have brought agriculture to this new land, enabling the growth of mainstay crops. This actually conflicts with the findings of scientists who believe Homo Sapiens walked to the Americas only via the Bering Land Bridge and the Cordilleran Ice Corridor.

50,000 and 140,000 year-old Amerindian skulls found in both California and Iran respectively, show that there has been inter-continental travel for a long time. What of the lost Amerindian civilization of Cahokia, complete with pyramids and a great wall? One site, near the present city of St. Louis, may have contained a metropolis of more than 250,000 North American Indians. And, who constructed the mysterious seven-mile walls of the Berkeley and Oakland, California, hills? Also, which pre-Mayan peoples engineered an elaborate waterworks in Yucatan to irrigate crops over 2000 years ago?

The Caracol Tower at Chichen Itza is a remarkable Mesoamerican observatory that seems to have correlated its findings with similar sites in North America, including Mesa Verde, Wichita, and Chaco Canyon. In contrast, Brad Steiger suggests in his book 'Worlds Before Our Own' that the cradle of civilization might possibly have travelled from the so-called New World to the Old.

How about the Homo Capensis? How long have they been around? From what I have read about those critters, if in fact they did or do exist, there are literally hundreds of their skulls surviving. I would assume other bones survived also. The skulls are unlike our human skulls in several ways. First, they have an elongated structure. The bone structure is thicker and heavier than human skulls. The cranial cavity is 25% to 33% larger than humans, indicating they may have had a larger brain and were consequently more intelligent than humans. Instead of the 3 parietal lobes that Homo sapiens have, the Homo Capensis has only 2 lobes. The eye sockets are larger and rounder and shallower than human eye sockets, and at the rear of the skull there are a hole or two that some surmise nerves or blood vessels passed through, possibly to nourish the larger brain. DNA has been obtained and tested, and the preliminary results indicate that these critters are NOT human, and if they did mate with a human, the first generation offspring would have been sterile. Now, here we are, into the 21st century, and we are just getting scientific evidence that Capensis exists. How many other critters exist in heaven, and on Earth, that we don't know about?

Scientists estimate that about 13.5 billion years have gone by since the Big Bang. How many other Big Bangs occurred prior, in the sea of time we call Eternity? It is impossible to tell what artifacts of the past still exist, and what may yet be discovered. To dismiss any possibility without investigation is the height of ignorance and arrogance.

Accordingly, if the "thinking man' or Homo-Sapiens were still the savages they are called at around 40,000 BCE, how can we explain the 50,000 year-old stairs carved out of stone found in Peru?

Recently, in December 2007, years after Ruth Shady Solis found the ancient city of Caral, Peru, scientists have accepted the carbon dating of 2,627 B.C.E., thereby establishing the civilization in South America to be much older than the Harappa Valley towns as well as the pyramids of Egypt. Many say that Caral must now be recognized as "the mother of all civilizations," the missing link of archaeology, the Mother City.

Perplexing Artefacts

Scientific knowledge has seemingly been prized by the inhabitants of every culture, known and unknown. Rock engravings, which may be as old as 60 million years, depict in step-by-step illustrations an entire heart-transplant operation and a Cesarean section. The ancient Egyptians used the equivalent of contraceptive jelly and had urine pregnancy tests. The cement used in filling Mayan dental cavities still holds after 1500 years.

No fabric is supposed to have been found until Egypt produced cloth material 5000 years ago. How should we take the Russian site which provides spindle whorls and patterned fabric designs over 80,000 years old?

The ancient Babylonians must also be included in these mysteries. Not only did the ancient Babylonians appear to use Sulphur matches, but they had a technology sophisticated enough to employ complex electrochemical battery cells complete with wiring. There is also evidence of electric batteries and electrolysis in ancient Egypt, India, and Swahililand.

Remains of a metal-working factory of over 200 furnaces were found at what is now Medzamor in Russian Armenia. Although a temperature of over 1780 degrees is required to melt platinum, some pre-Incan peoples in Peru were making objects of the metal. Even today the process of extracting aluminum from bauxite is a complicated procedure, but Zhou Chu, famous general of the Jin era (265-420 A.D.), was interred with aluminum belt fasteners on his burial costume.

Carved bones, chalk and stones, together with what appears to be greatly ornamented "coins," have been brought up from great depths during well-drilling operations. A strange, imprinted slab was found in a coal mine. The artefact was decorated with diamond-shaped squares with the face of an old man in each "box." In another coal-mine discovery, miners found smooth, polished concrete blocks which formed a solid wall. According to one miner's testimony, he chipped one block open to find the standard mixture of sand and cement that makes up most building blocks of today.

A gold necklace was found embedded in a lump of coal. A metal spike was discovered in a silver mine in Peru. An iron implement was found in a Scottish coal-bed, estimated to be millions of years older than man is believed to have existed. A metal, bell-shaped vessel, inlaid with a silver floral design was blasted out of solid rock near Dorchester, Massachusetts.

Two hypotheses may explain the presence of these perplexing artifacts: that they were manufactured by an advanced civilization on Earth which, due either to natural or technological catastrophe, was destroyed before our world's own genesis; or, that they are vestiges of a highly technological civilization of extraterrestrial origin, which visited this planet thousands, or even millions of years ago, leaving behind these various artifacts.

Even if a highly advanced extraterrestrial race might have visited this planet in prehistoric times, it seems unlikely such common, everyday items as nails, necklaces, buckles and vases would have been carried aboard a spacecraft and deposited in such widely separated areas; for such artifacts have been found in North and South America, Great Britain, the whole of Europe, Africa, Asia, and the Mid-East.

In a mysterious pyramid in China's Qinghai Province near Mount Baigong are three caves filled with pipes leading to a nearby salt-water lake. There are also pipes under the lake bed and on the shore. The iron pipes range in size, with some smaller than a toothpick. The strangest part is that they may be about

150,000 years old. Dating done by the Beijing Institute of Geology determined these iron pipes were smelted about 150,000 years ago, if they were indeed made by humans, according to Brian Dunning of Skeptoid.com. And, if they were made by humans, history as it is commonly viewed would have to be re-evaluated.

The dating was done using thermoluminescence, a technique that determines how long ago crystalline mineral was exposed to sunlight or heated. Humans are only thought to have inhabited the region for the past 30,000 years. Even within the known history of the area, the only humans to inhabit the region were nomads whose lifestyle would not leave any such structures behind. The state-run news agency Xinhua in China reported on the pyramid, the pipes, and the research began by a team scientists sent to investigate in 2002.

Though some have since tried to explain the pipes as a natural phenomenon, Yang Ji, a research fellow at the Chinese Academy of Social Sciences, told Xinhua the pyramid may have been built by intelligent beings. He did not dismiss the theory that ancient extraterrestrials may be responsible, saying this theory is "understandable and worth looking into … but scientific means must be employed to prove whether or not it is true." Another theory is that it was built by prehistoric humans with techniques lost to humans of a later period. The pipes lead into a salty lake, though a twin lake nearby contains freshwater. The surrounding landscape is strewn with what Xinhua described as "strangely shaped stones." Rocks protrude from the ground like broken pillars.

The head of the publicity department at the local Delingha government told Xinhua the pipes were analyzed at a local smeltery and 8 percent of the material could not be identified. The rest was made up of ferric oxide, silicon dioxide, and calcium oxide. The silicon dioxide and calcium oxide are products of long interaction between the iron and surrounding sandstone, showing the ancient age of the pipes. Liu Shaolin, the engineer who did the analysis, told Xinhua: "This result has made the site even more mysterious." "Nature is harsh here," he said. "There are no residents let alone modern industry in the area, only a few migrant herdsmen to the north of the mountain."

To further add to the mystery, Zheng Jiandong, a geology research fellow from the China Earthquake Administration told state-run newspaper People's Daily in 2007 that some of the pipes were found to be highly radioactive.

Pre-historic Nuclear Activity?

Large areas of fused green glass and vitrified cities have been found deep in the strata of archaeological digs at,

- Pierrelatte in Gabon, Africa
- The Euphrates Valley
- The Sahara Desert0

- The Gobi Desert
- Iraq
- The Mojave Desert
- Scotland
- The Old and Middle Kingdoms of Egypt
- South-central Turkey

In contemporary times, such material as fused green glass has only been known at nuclear testing sites (where the sand had melted to form the substance). It is quite unsettling to some to consider it possible that these sites provide evidence of a prehistoric nuclear war. At the same time, scientists have found a number of uranium deposits that appear to have been mined or depleted in antiquity.

The Great Pyramid (translated *fire in the middle*), is believed to have been built by Cheops, an African around 3760-3730 B.C. Was this also a nuclear reactor? If it is possible that nuclear annihilation of a global civilization did occur in prehistoric times, it seems even more urgent to learn who we really are before we find ourselves doomed to repeat the lessons left to us, by a world before our own.

Two Species?

There seem to be at least two different approaches to humanity, humankind and the designs of social co-existence. One is in the theme of cooperation, tolerance, acceptance, forgiveness, sacrifice and creation. The other is dominance, envy, conquering, and degradation, self-serving, vicious and destructive.

I contend that there are at least two species of man on the planet as indicated by the Bible. For example, Genesis 1:26-27 reads:

"26 Then God said, "Let us make mankind in our image, in our likeness, so that they may rule over the fish in the sea and the birds in the sky, over the livestock and all the wild animals, and over all the creatures that move along the ground."
27 So God created mankind in his own image, in the image of God he created them; male and female he created them."

When one reads Genesis further, (Gen. 2:7) one reads:

"And the Lord God molded Adam from the dust to resemble Himself,* and He blew on their faces the breath of life and Adam became a living soul."

For me, I always wondered why the writer would make the mistake of dividing this story into two parts – retelling the same story twice. There is also a fact of the Bible that when someone significant marries a family member, then it is clearly and unmistakably noted. For example:

"Isaac and Rebekah's firstborn son Esau married his cousin Mahalah, daughter of his father's brother Ishmael, while their second son Jacob married his cousins Leah and Rachel, daughters of his mother's brother Laban. The biblical character Amram married his paternal aunt, Jochebed, the mother of Miriam, Aaron and Moses."

These events were reported as they occurred and are completely clear and to the point. Why then doesn't it say that when Cain and Abel found wives that their wives were their sisters or cousins? And, if these were not members of the immediate 'Adam clan', from where did they come? It's a mystery for sure.

I conclude/contend that these are two different accounts, referring to the creation of 'Man', and then, the creation of 'Adam' (from whom comes Abraham, Isaac and Jacob – the first known Jews; also Ishmael - from whom the Arabs come) It is well known that these people were dark-complexioned with curly hair. Their characteristics were noted as being honest and forthright, as well as peaceful and helpful – governed by morality, faith and truth.

My ancestors, the Cherokee referred to these two species. They differentiated between 'Man' and 'Human Beings' – the difference being the humanity or compassion found in the latter. They also referred to 'Black Men' as well as 'White Men' having little or no humanity. It referred to these peoples having slaves and being excessively brutal. They made reference to their utter disregard for human life and Mother Earth.
If the first persons on the planet were made in God's image, and we know that some of the first inhabitants in our world were Black, this summation is an easy one. Even Jesus, who claimed to be "God in the flesh", was dark-skinned with curly hair. God could have come to Earth as anything - any color or species. Why a brown-skinned Jew?

It's a fact that the Elamites were African or, 'Kafir' (as it was known at the time), who came from Australia. From the 50,000 or so year-old statues and monoliths found all over the world – especially what is now known as Latin America, one can see that the world was inhabited, if not controlled by Afroid looking beings.

A BLACK THREAD

CHAPTER 3

ORIGINS

The earliest people in what we call the Americas are believed to have been of the Negritic African race,

3 ORIGINS

The Ethiopian

The Ethiopian was/is definitely one of the first races on the planet, which is evidenced by the more than 50,000 year-old statues bearing their likenesses found all over the world. These statues lend themselves to world exploration, and, quasi proves that those depicted were at least the rulers of the land, as no one would erect a statue to honor a commoner. The Sphynx also had deep Negroid features. This means that the rulers of at least part of the era during 50-70,000 BC, were black and therefore, the architects of at least part of our total existence. The fact that the Ethiopian existed much more than 50,000 years ago is evidenced by their language having been and still being spoken all over the world. When one adds that to those statues found in South America, and all over the world, then it becomes quite clear.

The earliest people in what we call the Americas are believed to have been the people of the Negritic African race, who are said to have entered the Americas as early as 100,000 years ago. They are believed to have come over by way of the Bearing Strait. It is also believed that a group of Africans left the then wet Sahara region via the Indian and Pacific Oceans from the East, and the Atlantic from the West. About 75,000 years ago, according to the Gladwin Thesis, black Pygmies, Negritic and Australoids peoples at different times, made this journey to the

Americas. The Austaloids were similar to the Aboriginals of Australia and Asia, including India as displayed by the ancient African terracotta portraits - 1000 B.C. to 500 B.C.

The Olmecs of Mexico, also known as the Xi People (is this a derivation of the name 'Zingh'?), according to recent language discoveries, originally came from West African Mende ethnicity. Mende script, written on ancient monuments found in Mexico was discovered to have been identical to the script used by the Mende people of West Africa.

Based on available information, it is my contention that the Black Olmecs or Mende arrived in America way before 1500 BCE as the monuments depicting them are believed by many to be much older.

The discovery of African cotton in North America further substantiates the fact that Africans, or those who traded with Africans, were present at the time. The only possibility of it arriving there is if someone brought it. The then wet Sahara, home of the fabled Zingh Empire, would have provided ample passage for crossing boats and ships carrying goods and products to America, and all around the world.

The genetic research by Sarah Tishkoff (Univ. of Maryland) suggests the DNA of the Ethiopian can also be found in the San, Kung and other East African groups separated by the Bantu expansion.

The Two Cradle Theory

Cheikh Anta Diop's (French anthropologist) 'Two Cradle Theory' postulates that the differences in today's societies evolved from two different models. One being the 'Southern Cradle-Egyptian Model' and the other, the 'Northern Cradle-Greek Model'.

Diop proposes that the characteristics of the 'Southern Cradle-Egyptian Model' include: the Abundance of vital resources; Sedentary-agricultural; Gentle, idealistic, peaceful nature with a spirit of justice; Matriarchal family; Emancipation of women in domestic life; Territorial state; Xenophilia; Cosmopolitanism; Social collectivism; Material solidarity of rights for individuals which makes moral or material misery unknown; Ideas of peace, justice, goodness and optimism; And, Literature emphasizing novel tales, fables and comedy.

In contrast, the characteristics of the Northern Cradle-Greek Model include: Bareness of resources; Nomadic-hunting (piracy); Ferocity or warlike nature fueled by a need to survive; Patriarchal family; Debasement or the enslavement of women.; City state (fort); Xenophobia; Parochialism; Individualism which promotes competition; Moral solitude; Disgust for existence, pessimism; and, Literature that favors tragedy and despair.

Both of these models are believed to have been drawn from the same blueprint, the types of which include hunting, fishing, herding, and farming.

How does one recognize the years 2400-2200 BCE as the beginning of civilization when there exists evidence of cities, hunting, and irrigation from over 12,000 years ago – maybe even 100 thousand years ago? Who makes those decisions? For example, even though at the time there was only a jaw-bone, a piece of a finger and a piece of a skull, we accepted that the Denisovans existed. The Denisovans have been called the missing link, a sub-species found in Northern Russia and are said to have been giants. In contrast, there are thousands of fragments in the Sahara or thereabouts that validate the existence of the Zingh Empire but historians and experts still say their existence is in question.

The Zingh Empire

The Zingh Empire is said to have existed about fifteen thousand years ago. The Zingh Dynasty was a "Negritic civilization composed of Pygmies." The only other civilizations that may have been in existence at that period in history were the Ta-Seti civilization of what became Nubia-Kush and the mythical Atlantis civilization which may have existed out in the Atlantic, off the coast of West Africa (or Bermuda) about ten to fifteen thousand years ago. That raises the question as to whether there was a relationship between the prehistoric Zingh Empire of West Africa and the civilization of Atlantis, whether the Zingh Empire was actually Atlantis, or whether Atlantis if it existed was part of the Zingh Empire. Was Atlantis, the highly technologically sophisticated civilization an extension of Black civilization in the Meso-America and other parts of the Americas?

The ancient West African coastal and interior Kingdoms occupied an area that is now covered with dense vegetation but may have been cleared about three to four thousand years ago. This includes the regions from the coasts of West Africa to the South, all the way inland to the Sahara. A number of large kingdoms and empires existed in that area. According to Blisshords Communications, one of the oldest empires and civilizations on earth existed just north of the coastal regions into what is today Mauritania. The Zingh Empire was the first to use the red, black and green African flag and to plant it throughout their territory all over Africa and the world.

The Green Sahara

During the "Green Sahara" period, around 8000-7000 BCE to about 3500-3000 BCE, it is widely believed that this aquatic civilization of the Zingh Empire existed there, and, is widely recognized, well-known and repeated in the African oral tradition. This period was also known as the Neolithic Subpluvial. In this time, the region was moist and wet, which supported abundant flora and therefore, also supported a thriving human population. Also during this time, large areas of North, East, West and Central Africa exhibited hydrographic biodiversity that offered nurturing living conditions for its human inhabitants.

This time hosted a completely different landscape. For

example, the lakes were much higher than today – by tens of meters. They also had different drainages. Lake Chad covered an area of about 250,000 square miles (roughly 400,000 kilometers) with a sea level 100 feet higher than today, and Lake Turkana ran off into the Nile River basin. In this subpluvial era existed many shallow lakes which today can only be detected with radar or through satellite imagery.

As this was the period before agriculture, the abundance of fish, waterfowl and water associated animals, the result of the increased moisture and water, offered ready sustenance for the indigenous human population. The natural transformation from hunting to the river way of life supported a much larger and wider population, promoting expansion.

The excavations by British archaeologist Anthony Arkell reveal that the skeletal remains found prove that these people were related to the modern Nilotic peoples which include the Nuer and Dinka peoples. The evidence of grain cultivation suggests that this culture had a pivotal role in moving civilization from a vegeculture to an agriculture.

The bone harpoons and wavy-line pottery found there indicate a hunting and fishing culture existed in around 7500 BCE. Renowned archaeologist Gabriel Camps postulated the pottery found in the region belonged to an African culture rather than the previously believed 'Mediterranean' inhabitants. Camps also found that instead of the gathering of wild grains, there was evidence of the cultivation of grain crops. This evidence that proves the transition from hunting and fishing, and then vegeculture to farmers, proves that whatever culture did live there, lived there long enough to have thrived and advanced. The primarily aquatic culture is also evidenced in the findings of Professor Paul Sereno in the northeastern Niger region known as Gobero. Here, the remains of the Kiffian (7700-6200 BCE) and Tenerian (5200-2500 BCE) cultures were well preserved.

The bones of fish, as well as tools and other implements from 10,000 years ago, mainly harpoon-heads, point to boating and other water-related activities. It is believed, based on the hunting practices of today's Songhai (who still use harpoons to hunt hippopotamuses), that the harpoons dating 9000 years ago were used for the same purpose.

It could be said of the Zingh Dynasty that the transition from hunter, to fisher to herder and finally farmer, was inherently dependent upon the wetlands that previously existed in that region circa 7000 BCE. It could also be deduced that their culture's decline was facilitated by the drying up of these wetlands and waterways. This 'dryer' weather would have reduced the availability of natural flora and vegetation, probably prompting the need for agriculture and irrigation.

The Akkadian Influence: Arabs and Jews

Let's examine the Semites, the Arabs and Jews of old. They were of brown skin as well, and are both known to contain CMH (Cohen Modal Haplotype) The Cohen Modal Haplotype is a characteristic Y chromosome haplotype used to trace Jewish ancestral origins of various populations. For more than a decade, it has been known that many self-proclaimed Jewish priests carry the CMH. To summarize, the CMH indicates that a great many contemporary Jewish priests are descended from a limited number of paternal lineages.

Let's look at the Akkadian language. This, a now extinct East Semitic language, was spoken in Mesopotamia and used the cuneiform writing system. It is the earliest known Semitic language, it is said to be a part of the greater Afro-asiatic language family, originally used to write ancient Sumerian. Although it is said to have been named after the city of Akkad, (a major center of Mesopotamian civilization during the Akkadian Empire, ca. 2334–2154 BCE), it predates the city by many hundreds of years.

It is a fact that the Jews and Muslims of this time were brown or Black. Is it safe to say that if the language was Semitic, then the culture was Jewish? So, if the Akkadian and Sumerian influenced the Persian as well as the Greek cultures and language, and European culture is a product of the Greeks, it is safe to say that black or brown people influenced civilization as we know it today. When one understands that the Jews of this time were at least brown, isn't it safe to say that the issues they had stemmed from this condition?

There seems to be a question about whether or not the original Muslims and Jews were black. Even though 'race' seems to be more of a contemporary focus or concern, history and the past reveals the truth through modern technology.

From a historical standpoint, we cannot ignore the proof that many Muslims were Moors. The Moor, as well as the Jew has been the target of the Roman Catholic Church for quite some time. The Torah, Koran and Bible all speak of Abraham, who was the father of Isaac and Ismael. Isaac is the father of the Jew, and Ishmael, the father of the Muslim. That makes the Jew and the Muslim blood relatives from the same family.

The Sumerian and Akkadian cultures that influenced it gave it the characteristics of a sprachbund or combined language. The earliest found texts are believed to be dated at around 2500 BCE. To date, many thousands of texts have been found chronicling legal texts, correspondence, scientific texts, military and political events, and mythological stories. It is also important to note that both Mesopotamian nations' languages, Assyrian and Babylonian, were both forms of the Akkadian language.

Many of the languages in the Far East were influenced by Akkadian due to the dominating Mesopotamian empires. These include the Akkadian Empire, Babylonian Empire, Middle Assyrian Empire and of course, the Akkadian Empire itself. Around the 8th century BC, during the Neo-Assyrian Empire and the reign of Tiglath-Pileser III, the Akkadian language began its decline, as it was being marginalized by

Aramaic. The Hellenistic period saw the language primarily being used by priests and scholars in the temples of Assyria and Babylonia.

Between the 3rd and 2nd millennium BC, Akkadian gradually replaced Sumerian as a spoken language. This bilingualism spurred the development of an intimate cultural symbiosis between the two cultures.
The fall of the Akkadian Empire saw the people of Mesopotamia divide into two major Akkadian-speaking nations: Assyria in the north, and, centuries later, Babylonia in the south.

Modern history begins at Sumer because the Sumerians were undoubtedly the first to have a functioning system of writing. The origins of this are now plausibly explained by Denise Schmandt-Besserat (cf. Before Writing, Volume I, From Counting to Cuneiform [University of Texas Press, 1992]). For purposes of accounting, contracts, shipping, etc., little clay models were made of the kinds of commodities involved. For convenience, these models were then placed in clay wrappers. Then, so that the contents of the wrappers could be known without breaking them, little drawings of the models began to be put on the wrappers. Soon it became obvious that the little drawings by themselves made the models superfluous.
Since the Crusades were about a war being waged on these same Muslims and Jews, it can also be deducted that this too was about not only religion, but also about race. During that time in history, the cities inhabited by Muslims or under Muslim rule allowed Christian and Jewish faiths, along with Buddhists and Hindus to co-

exist and thrive alongside their religion without incident.

The Muslims and Jews of that day had to have been predominantly people of color, or at least brown skin. This conclusion can be arrived at because the region from which they came was northern Africa.

This Black Presence

The history of the black man is steeped in royalty. They were rulers and kings, slave owners and lawmakers. They were the Elamites, Persians and the Egyptians who ruled with blood and fear. They were the Muslim, Jewish and Christian Moors who brought civilization to Europe. The royal bloodlines of King James and the family Stuart and Maurice ruled over Europe during the 1500-1700's.

Now, let's understand what it is with which we are dealing. The Angles occupied Britain circa 500 A. D. until the arrival of the Saxons. The mingling of these two is what gives us the Anglo-Saxon. So yes, the Brits are German, which explains why English is a Germanic language. This is also why Prince Harry is proud to display his German roots by wearing Nazi costumes. Just look at the name 'England'. The German word for narrow is 'eng', so I believe the name England is German for 'narrow land'.

During the First World War with Germany, anti-German sentiment threatened the stability of Great Britain, as many Brits were of German descent. King

George V became the first monarch of the House of Windsor, which he changed from the House of Saxe-Coburg and Gotha. The British royal family at that time was called Saxe-Coburg and Gotha, from the long reigning dynasty of the Saxon House of Wettin, the same family who ruled Belgium, France and the Netherlands. George V's first cousins at that time included Tsar Nicholas II of Russia and Kaiser Wilhelm II of Germany. During this tumultuous conflict between brethren, (much like the American Civil War), fear of reprisal caused them to change their name. They then adopted the name of the Castle Windsor, and are still known by that name.

The Anglo-Saxon missionaries knew of the superstitions and morality of the Afroids and therefore, brought them an omnipotent icon to control and govern them. They could then have willing slaves who gladly entered into, and stayed in servitude – for their entire lives. In the beginning, the Africans had the gold, diamonds and silver and the missionaries had the bibles. In just a few short years, the missionaries had the gold, silver and diamonds and the Africans had the bibles."

The Quest for Power

Pope Urban II wanted more political power, and, to advance the control of the Roman Catholic Church through Christianity, so he made an unmistakable target. It is my belief that the same fear of a growing, thriving non-white population fueled the Crusades as much as the topic of religion. This is evidenced by the fact that even those Muslims and Jews who converted to Christianity, becoming devout Christians were also killed by Christians during the Crusades.

I'm not suggesting that all Muslims observed their rules of law and treated others with proper respect, but many did. Theirs was an existence of cooperation and tolerance toward others. They would however, defend themselves and their families to the death when threatened. The fact that they weren't easily conquered brought fear and anger to those who wanted to subject the whole world to the tyranny of this version of this new Christian regime.

How can we know what happened at that time? The Christians give one account of Muslim and Jewish activity at that time, and the Muslims and Jews have a totally different perspective. This scenario is also true in the reverse. The religious freedom offered by both the Muslim and Jewish faiths may have posed a threat to the desired activity of the Roman Catholic Church.

Visual History

Artists throughout time have at least two sources for their work. It is either based on imagination – seeing from the mind's eye, or a rendering of what exists before our eyes. We covet what we see. That brings to mind the Venus of Willendorf found in Austria. It was carved by a Negro sculptor of the Grimaldi race 10,000 to 15,000 years ago and possesses the unmistakable characteristics of an African Bush woman. That means that more than 10,000 years ago, Negros had the tools and capability to carve stone. The Grimaldi were a Negroid race who lived in Europe as late as 12,000 years ago. Many traces of their culture have been found in Southern and Central Europe. Even two full Grimaldi skeletons are in the Museum of Monaco near Monte Carlo.

The Olmecs also built mud pyramids in Mexico and created Terracotta art showing common activities such as pottery making and wrestling. Around 3100 BCE, the Olmecs also made an accurate calendar system.
Indus Kush Civilization

The presence of Black people in ancient and modern India is well documented by historian Runoko Rashidi . He stated On March 3, 2000, during a lecture in Honolulu, Hawaii, that the face of India changed around 2000 B.C. when nomadic people of Indo-European or Aryan origin traveled to the Innis Valley and other fertile locations in Southern India. Author Wayne Chandler in his book "African Presence in Early Asia." spoke of Harrappa and Mohenjo-daro - two of the many cities built by Black people, that cover large regions of northern India and modern-day Pakistan.

The Minoans Ancient Greece

Manfred Bietak, noted Archaeologist, researched ancient Greek civilizations and their connections to ancient Egypt. Bietak found artwork as early as 7000 B.C. that shows that the early people inhabiting Greece were of African descent. Known for their vibrant cities, opulent palaces and established trade connections, this Minoan culture of Ancient Greece reached its peak at about 1600 B.C. Minoan ruins reveal the sophistication of paved roads and even piped water systems. In art history, Minoan Bronze age artwork is recognized as a major era of visual achievement. Pottery, sculptures and frescoes from the Minoans are displayed in museums all over the world.

Shang Dynasty of Ancient China

The first African is believed to have arrived in China about 60,000 years ago according to a genetic study published in the *"Proceedings of the National Academy of Science Genetic,"*. Li Jin , researcher and population geneticist states, "Our work shows that modern humans first came to southeast Asia and then moved later to northern China. This supports the idea that modern humans originated in Africa."

According to Nibs Ra and Manu Amun, authors of the essay from the *"Light Words from the Dark Continent; A Collection of Essays,"* (published 2009), the first documented governance in China was headed by the Shang (or Chiang) dynasty in 1500-1000 B.C.E. The founder of the Shang dynasty, King T'ang (or Ta), was of African descent. The Shang were also called Nakhi, which literally means "Black" (Na) and "Man" (khi). History states that the Shang dynasty, under the rule of King T'ang was responsible for unifying China – enabling them to form their first civilization.

Ancient Mesopotamia

It is the belief of many scholars that Black Sumerians were the founders of the first Mesopotamian civilization. Mesopotamia (Biblical Shinar or Sumer), is said to have come into existence at around 3000 B.C.E. Henry Rawlinson after researching ancient Mesopotamia for many years, deciphered the cuneiform script and discovered that the founders of the civilization were of Kushite (or Cushite) origin.
He also found that the Semitic speakers of Akkad along with the non-Semitic speakers of Sumer were both Black people who called themselves sag-gig-ga or "Black Heads."

In his book *"PreHistoric Nations"* (1869) John Baldwin: wrote "The early colonists of Babylonia were of the same race as the inhabitants of the Upper Nile."
Many other scholars, including, Chandra Chakaberty, agreed with Baldwin. In his book *"A Study in Hindu Social Polity"* Chakaberty, asserted that "based on the statuaries and steles of Babylonia, the Sumerians were "of dark complexion (chocolate color), short stature, but of sturdy frame, oval face, stout nose, straight hair, full head; they typically resembled the Dravidians, not only in cranium, but almost in all the details."

Sources:
(PreHistoric Nations by John D. Baldwin, New York: Harper & Brothers, 1869, pg. 192), (A Study in Hindu Social Polity by Chandra Chakaberty, Delhi: Mittal Publications, 1987, pg. 33), (From Babylon to Timbuktu by Rudolph R. Windsor. Atlanta: Windsor's

Golden Series, 2203)

Elam, an African civilization of Persia that flourished around 2900 B.C., is said to have been older than Egypt or Ethiopia. The capital of Elam was Susa, the same Susa of Xerxes in the book of Esther of the Bible. During the 12th year of the reign of Xerxes, (an African), Haman, because of perceived disrespect from Mordecai, Esther's uncle, sought to destroy the Jews in Elam.

It then becomes the hidden fact that some Africans, because of jealousy and fear, hated the Jew. The Jews are direct descendants of Adam or Adamos – whom God made from the dust and infused with a touch of the divine. Throughout time, many Africans have sought to destroy the Jew: enslaving them, as well as selling them into bondage from the time of Elam, well into the 20th century. Many will argue this fact and cite biblical verse but the true facts remain. The blacks who were slaves in Africa and the first sold to the Europeans as slaves were Jews.

Please understand that this is not 'African-bashing' or blind support of the Jew or Muslim, just facts about history that seemed to have been hidden, lost or simply ignored.

Data Analysis

What do all the above mentioned facts, or conjecture have to do with the concept of this book? It is a known fact that the majority of those who existed during these times of discovery, pre-history and history were people of color. It is my belief that this is where the thread begins.

My contention is that people of African descent, (be they African, Muslim, Asian or Jewish), or at least, brown people, were responsible for, and therefore co-architects of, our current world. Throughout/during many of the most significant events in world history, many of the citizens, as well as rulers of those countries were Afroid.

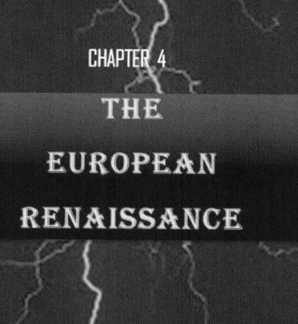

CHAPTER 4

THE

EUROPEAN

RENAISSANCE

the highly visible rock form was named *Djibal Tarik* (Tarik's Mountain), or Gibraltar as we know it today.

4 THE EUROPEAN RENAISSANCE

The Moors: Light of Europe's Dark Age

The European Renaissance was initiated and/or inspired by the Moors - who brought knowledge, mathematics, science and culture from the Byzantine Empire to Europe and beyond. The Moors can therefore be said to have brought civilization and humanity to the Western world.

For example, when the Moors came to Europe, they found pestilence and plagues. Existing schools were only for the very elite, so the average person couldn't read or write. There was little hygiene as animals lived in, and had free range of, family homes – the source of many of the illnesses in the regions at the time. Even the word 'stall' is a Moorish word meaning '*The place one keeps animals*'.

Also, the African apparently arrived in the new world without disease, as their constitution lent itself to almost perfect health. They had no TB, syphilis or any other venereal diseases. The African missionary Livingstone along with a medical doctor wrote that "*Syphilis dies out in the African interior. It seems incapable of permanence in any form in persons of pure African blood.*" It is said that syphilis originated in Europe around 1494 – believed to have been brought by those who sailed with Columbus. Just like today with AIDS and Ebola viruses, the powers that be have blamed those of African descent, saying that the diseases come from them.

Origin of the Word Moor

The name Moor was used to refer to these dark-skinned North Africans of Arab and/or Berber origin in antiquity and medieval Western Europe. These Moors were the Muslims who created and then, inhabited Islamic Spain, or, as it was otherwise known, Al-Andalus. But, where did this word originate?
The word 'Moor' comes from the word '*Mauri*'. This word Mauri previously referred to the tribes from the Roman provinces of Mauretania, which today are known as western Algeria and northeastern Morocco. In Middle Age Latin, Mauri described a mixture of Berbers and Arabs of the coastal regions of Northwest Africa. In Spain, Portugal, and Italy, the word Mauri changed into Moros.

According to the Oxford English Dictionary, the Moors, as early as the Middle Ages and as late as the 17th century, were "commonly supposed to be black or very swarthy, and hence the word is often used for Negro." For a long period the Dutch language used Moor and Moriaan for Black Africans and in modern Liberia, the name Moryan is still prominent. From its inception, up to, and beyond the fourteenth century, the English attached racial connotation to it to describe black people. To this day, those racial connotations remain.

In addition, Muslims are often referred to as *'the Mudejares'* and *'the Moriscos'* terms given to all Muslims who stayed in Spain after their persecution and worked for the Christian nobles. The Muslims who fought their Muslim brothers with the Christians were called 'mudajjal' and, when the Mudejares were forced to be baptized, they became known as Moriscos, or the Christian Moors.

Given today's representation of the Muslim, there seems to be a question of the ethnicity of the ,Moors who conquered Spain. I, myself have seen representations that would rival Northern Europeans. For those who doubt the ethnicity of these particular Muslims, eyewitness accounts are as follows: *"Their faces were black as pitch, the handsomest amongst them was as black as a cooking pot."*

Origin of the Moors' Presence in Europe

The study of the African presence in history, whether in the African Diaspora or Africa itself, is enriching and rewarding. In this study we realize that slavery alone is not African history and that African history is everybody's history. The history of African/Black people is rich and comprehensive, inspiring and, often, little known. Nowhere is this more the case than the African presence in Medieval and Renaissance Europe.

The seventh and eighth centuries saw North Africa being invaded by the Arabs. This surge of Islam was adopted into Moorish culture and they, crossing over from Morocco to the Iberian Peninsula, experienced legendary victories brought forth by incredible feats of valor. For, example Tarif, after whom the important southern Spanish port city is named, with a cast of 400 Berbers and 100 horses in 710 AD, carried out a most important introductory mission, which opened the door for those who followed.

The Moors in Spain

The Moorish conquest of Spain however can be attributed to Tarik bin Ziyad who commanded an army of 10,000 men. Year 711 saw Tarik, a Muslim, cross the straits near a well-known rock promontory. As a result his victory over the Europeans in that area/passage, the highly visible rock form was named *Djibal Tarik* (Tarik's Mountain), or Gibraltar as we know it today. Armed with fortitude and the knowledge of the ancients, he and his band of warriors took control of Iberian Peninsula in only about a month. Since then, the Moorish legacy became an inextricable episode of the Spanish history. The words spoken by Tarik bin Ziyad believed to have inspired his followers to victory were:

"My brethren, the enemy is before you, the sea is behind; whither would ye fly? Follow your general; I am resolved either to lose my life or to trample on the prostrate king of the Romans."

These Muslim Moors who originally arrived in Spain in 711 C.E were mainly the aforementioned Arabs and Berbers of North Africa. By 770 C.E. people of all races from North Africa and Arabia migrated to Andalusia corresponding to Spain and Portugal at that time. Intermarriages occurred with various nationalities including the native Spanish-Muslim population. During the reign of Abdur-Rahman, (755-

788), these people began the work of building an Islamic civilization equivalent to the one already existing in Damascus and Baghdad. After invading Spain in 711 BCE, the Islamic culture they established lasted more the 700 years. Within the span of a century, they managed to develop a unique civilization far in advance of the civilization existing in Europe at the time. The most popular name for these Muslims who lived in Spain is 'the Moors.'

In true revolutionary fashion, these Moors and Jews, who held control over the important Iberian Peninsula, were usurped and ousted by solders on behalf of King Ferdinand and the young Queen Isabella. After the expulsion of the Moors by the Christians from Granada in 1492 (5 years after the beginning of the Spanish Inquisition which involved the torture and murder of Muslims and Jews), over 3.5 million Moors and Jews were banished due to their apparent threat to Christianity. Many were tortured in order to force them to renounce their religions, which, many did, converting to the Christian faith. Between 1492 and 1610, over 4 million Muslims and Jews were expelled from the region by King Manuel of Portugal and subsequently, by King Phillip III of Spain.

They did however leave an indelible mark on that society both genetically and culturally in the forms of religion and Morisco descendants. Many of who settled in France and Holland. In fact, the story in the Netherlands of, *Zwarte Piet'*, or Black Pete, is based on a Moorish orphan boy whom ,*Sinterklaas*' or Santa Claus adopted and trained as his assistant.

Moorish Heroes

The Black Saint Maurice: Knight of the Holy Lance

However few, as we said before, there are at least *some* representations of Black leaders and Blacks of nobility in Europe. In some places, one can actually see depictions of Black Mary and Jesus, as well as Black apostles. Still, during my 20 years traversing Europe, it is very rare that I see representations of the Moors or other Black people who may have ruled and/or governed Europe.

That being said, of all those many Black men in the history of Europe, few have excited the imagination more than Saint Maurice. The Black Saint Maurice (the Knight of the Holy Lance) is the great patron saint of the Holy Roman Germanic Empire. In Germany, he is known as '*Saint Mauritius*'.

He was a Black saint in an area that then and now, has had very few Black inhabitants. The actual name Maurice comes from Latin and actually means "like a Moor." He was also a Black knight. Indeed, we could call him a knight in shining armor and he was no less than remarkable.

The earliest version of the Maurice story and the account upon which all later versions are based, is found in the writings of Bishop Eucherius of Lyons, who lived more than 1500 years ago. According to Eucherius, Saint Maurice was a high official in the Thebaid region of Southern Egypt — a very early center of Christianity.

Maurice, a true Negro was the commander of a Roman legion of Christian soldiers. Stationed in Africa, he and his contingent of 6,600 men were dispatched to Gaul, Switzerland in 287 AD. to suppress a Christian uprising by the decree of Roman emperor Maximian Herculius. Maurice disobeying the order, chose to die rather than persecute Christians. He was ordered to be killed by Emperor Maximian because of his refusal to attack the Christians. As a result, he and almost all of his troops were martyred when they refused to renounce their faith and sacrifice to the gods of the Romans. They were executed in the year 290-300 in Switzerland near a place that would later become Saint Maurice-en-Valais.

To understand the impact this Moor, now the Celestial Saint of Germany, had on this nation that would one day focus on race, one must know with whom his name and legacy are associated. These include: Charlemagne, the grandson of Charles Martel; the most distinguished representative of the Carolingian dynasty; Otto I; and, Cardinal Albert of Brandenburg;

Countries and cities that still see him as their patron saint include: Switzerland, Northern Italy, Burgundy, and along the Rhine. This includes the major cities of Tours, Angers, Lyons, Chalon-sur-Saone, Dijon, Magdeburg and Halle, Germany, and, also in the Baltic States, where merchants in Tallin and Riga also adopted his iconography. The House of the Black Heads of Riga, whose seal bore the distinct image of a

Moor's head, have a wooden statuette of St. Maurice. By 1000 C.E. the worship of Maurice was only rivaled by St. George and St. Michael. He is often depicted with an Eagle above his head. It is also of note that many portrayals of Hitler (some 1700 years later) also show *him* with what seems to be the same Eagle above his head.

His significance is such that after the second half of the 12th century, the emperors were appointed by the Pope in front of the altar of St. Maurice, in St. Peter's Cathedral in Rome.

Black Kings in the Art of the European Renaissance

When one knows Europe, one knows that there are very few representations and images of Black leadership in early Europe, well into medieval times. Included in these rare depictions are multiple renditions of the Black Magus (or king), Balthazar, who is often mistaken for a Muslim, but who, is said to have become a Christian. He is one of the three wise men whose face and stature is depicted by thousands of representations all over the world. He is said to have come from Ethiopia and was to have brought Guggul or 'Myrrh' as it is more commonly known. Sometimes, particularly in the Dutch world, another of the kings is identified as Black. This is Gaspar, identified as a king from Asia and he is also credited sometimes as bringing myrrh, and sometimes frankincense.

Some of these higher ranks led to leadership positions

like Sir Morien, the Black Night who was claimed to have been in King Arthur's Round Table. The quintessential knight, his bravado is well documented. He is said to have been one of the most virtuous, and bravest knights of antiquity and in English prose, he is often compared to Lancelot himself. He is credited with saving the life of Sir Gawain on the field of battle as well and came to personify all of the finest virtues of the knights of medieval Europe. His knowledge and articulate speech were also lauded.

Sharing the Wealth of Knowledge

Assimilation into European Culture

Concerning the role of the Moors in the European Renaissance, let's be perfectly clear. The Moor is known to have learned from, as well as influenced, Greek culture. They were not only the conveyors of Greek heritage and culture, but rather refiners and creators, co-responsible for the foundations of Western Science.

In the Middle East, many classical Greek texts, especially the works of Aristotle, were translated into Syriac during the 6th and 7th centuries by Nestorian, Melkite or Jacobite monks living in Palestine, or by Greek exiles from Athens or Edessa who visited Islamic centers of higher learning. The Islamic world then kept, translated, and developed many of these texts, especially in centers of learning such as Baghdad, where a "House of Wisdom" with thousands of manuscripts existed as early as 832. These texts were in turn translated into Latin in the Middle Ages by scholars such as Michael Scot (who made translations of '*Historia Animalium*' and '*On the Soul*' as well as of Averroes's commentaries). During the 11th and 12th centuries, Eastern Christians played an important role in exploiting this knowledge, especially through the Christian Aristotelian School of Baghdad.

As a result, many of these Moors had extensive knowledge of philosophy, languages (both written and spoken), mathematics, art and science. This made them seem more advanced than the typical European and therefore, preferred candidates for select high-end positions of responsibility. So, once expelled from Spain or Portugal, it was not uncommon for them to be placed into positions of authority. Along with these positions came wealth and influence which we will discuss later in this chapter. Many Moors began to settle in the surrounding areas, including, Belgium, Luxembourg, Germany, England and other neighboring countries. As a matter of fact, so many began to migrate to England that in 1596, Queen Elizabeth is quoted with having written:

"There are of late divers Blakamores brought into this realm, of which kinde of people there are already too manie."

Innovation and Advancement

Strategic Advantage: Paper and Gunpowder

Two of the most important and empowering

innovations of the Middle Ages were paper and gunpowder. Paper because it allowed the culture to advance through written example with translations of Greek and Arabic texts in astronomy and mathematics, as well as science and medicine. The introduction of paper via the Silk Road allowed the Muslims to supply Europe ideas and information. It also made remote communication possible so that ideas and messages could be carried from kingdom to kingdom, even by the common man. It also allowed the histories of the common man to be written down - replacing the oral traditions of storytelling.

Gunpowder was one of the most important tactical innovations of the period because it eliminated the need for hand-to-hand combat − allowing remote handling of opponents. It gave its possessor technological strategic advantage in battle as it could be used as a demolition device against enemy's strongholds, as well as simultaneously eliminating entire groups of opponents. It is said that black powder changed the balance of power forever, giving its possessor dominance. These culture-changing innovations were given to Europe by the Moors.

More Islamic innovations during the Islamic Golden Age also included the arts, agriculture, alchemy, music, pottery, and many other cultural and societal components. Add to those Arabic loan words which include the star name Aldebaran, scientific terms such as algebra, algorithm and alchemy (from where we get chemistry), and, names such as sugar, camphor, cotton, and other commodities, and we see the beginnings of modern culture. Paper and gunpowder however, remain two of the most important of all these innovations.

Combined Cultures

There were many important contact points between Europe and the Islamic lands during the middle Ages. Following the conquest of the city by Spanish Christians in 1085, Sicily and in Spain, particularly Toledo, were two of the main conduits through which important knowledge was transferred. The year 1091 in the Norman-Arab-Byzantine culture saw Islamic cartographers, poets, soldiers and scientists in the court of King Roger II. The Crusades also perpetuated interaction between Europe and the Levant, by way of Italian maritime republics. Arab and Latin cultures blended seamlessly in Levant cities like Antioch.

A great many Christian scholars travelled to Muslim lands to learn sciences in the 11th and 12th centuries including Leonardo Fibonacci, Adelard of Bath and Constantine the African. From the 11th to the 14th centuries, students from all over the world also studied medicine, cosmography, philosophy, mathematics, and other subjects in these "universities".

So, in essence, these 'Blackamoors' helped spur the growth of Europe even beyond its shores. These advancements are well documented and recognized by historians all over the world. People of color did in fact contribute more to Europe's development than for which some are willing to give them credit. That these

Moorish contributions would be ignored by Europe is ironic as without this Islamic intervention, the European Renaissance may never have occurred, or at least been extensively delayed.

Indirect Moorish Impact on America

America is said to be the child of the Middle Ages and the mother of Modern Times. This is clearly evidenced in older cities in America that were founded by Europeans. The customs, dwellings, schools, churches and even city and street names validate this idea. Re-thinking the Moorish stimulus to European Renaissance is basically reinterpreting the link between the two ages and investigating its impact on subsequent European and American enterprises namely: Columbus's voyage to the New World. It is fair to say that the Middle Ages were the precursor of Modern Times. It is fallacious however, to consider that these Middle Ages were *only* dark because the thousand years before the Renaissance boasted many advancements, as well as great accomplishments.

The concepts of Plato and Aristotle brought by the Moors helped drive the European Renaissance, influencing the morality and especially, the language. Other advances that can be directly attributed to the Moorish influence include Astronomy and mathematics.

The Moorish influence on European culture and development is well-known. This influence includes shining non-tangible examples as well as hands-on intervention. If one closely examines the American culture, one will, find social structure similar to that of Europe during the renaissance.

The Classical and Scientific Renaissance

The Middle Ages, or ‚Dark Ages' ushered in an era of philosophical thought and this way of thinking became the raw material for the European Scientific Revolution. This essential knowledge was shared with the West through the Iberian Peninsula in so that the Moorish scientific genius became an impetus to the subsequent European development. Also, the impact the Moors had on European literature, as well as science was very significant as it also helped trigger European expansion. This Moor-influenced scientific development is believed to have been what prompted Columbus to sail west to reach the East.

The Moors stimulated the Classical Renaissance of Europe relating to literature and art. They also launched the Scientific Renaissance of the 12th and 13th centuries with the discoveries of the Arabs and the Moors, which constituted the foundations of Western Science. It can be deduced then that the classical and scientific renaissance in Europe was a direct result of the Moorish stimulus.

The Islamic inhabitation of Spain created schools of translation through which the culture was made available to the rest of Europe and the world. The Christian Crusades also brought Moorish science to the masses as an impetus for change.

It is a little-known fact, but in the Middle Ages, many Islamic cities in the Middle East, including Cordoba, Cairo, Damascus and Baghdad, were considered the centers of civilization, while Europe was still living in the "Dark Ages". While Muslim Spain was benefitting from the science revolution, Europeans saw science as witchcraft and sorcery, and therefore, rejected it. Europe was considered backward and uncultured as it had little organization and hardly any infrastructure.

The article 'How Islam influenced the European Renaissance' by Karima Saifullah, reveals that *"in the ninth century, the library of the monastery of St. Gall was the largest in Europe having only 36 volumes. During this same period, Cordoba's library contained over 500,000!"*

Studying at colleges was first applied by Muslims as universities were established in Muslim countries in the late 600s and the early 700s, while leading colleges, like Oxford and the University of Paris, were founded at least 600 years later. Even the classification of student class levels, i.e., 'Undergraduate' and 'Graduate' (mutafaqqih and Sahib, respectively), have their roots directly in the Islamic educational systems. Cordoba, capital of Muslim Spain, well-known for its scientific advances, enticed students from all over the world to come and study.

Direct Influence

Let's examine specifically some of the many ways Moors directly influenced the European Renaissance.

Hospitals

Today's model for the hospital can be directly traced back to Islamic culture from the Middle Ages as there was one in every major Islamic city. The hospital in Cairo boasted more than 8000 beds, offering separate wards for fevers, ophthalmic, dysentery and surgical cases. The discovery of the origin of smallpox can be attributed to doctor Al Rhazes who also proved that one could only get it once in her or his lifetime. This was significant because it proved the existence and function of the immune system. Rhazes is also considered the father of pediatrics, and, a pioneer in neurosurgery and ophthalmology. He is also considered by some to have been the greatest physician of Islam and the Medieval Ages. How ironic that the Christian Crusaders relied upon Arab doctors on many occasions for medical related issues.

Medicine

Islamic Moors also had major impact on European medicine and medical practices. Al-Razi and Ibn Sina were two of the main sources for Gerard of Cremona's translations - Receuil des traités de médecine.

Even Europe's standard medical journal was translated from an Islamic work and his work, Avicenna's The Canon of Medicine was translated into Latin, disseminated in manuscript and printed form, and, was published at least thirty-five times. It was here wherein he described the contagious nature of some infectious diseases which he said were left in the air by the sick.

In this publication, he also discussed how to effectively test new medicines and treatments. He is also credited for writing another well-known textbook in Europe, The Book of Healing, a general encyclopedia of science and philosophy.

Other medical publications include the Comprehensive Book of Medicine from Muhammad ibn Zakarīya Rāzi. It is noted for its distinction between measles and smallpox, which was also prevalent in Europe, and, a clear description of the two.

Abu al-Qasim al-Zahrawi's Kitab al-Tasrif was an encyclopedia of medicine, known for its section on surgery and descriptions and diagrams of surgical instruments, many of which he developed. Specifically, the section on surgery was later translated to Latin again by Gerard of Cremona, reprinted and used in European medical schools until the late 1700's.

Literature

As previously stated, the phenomenon of paper allowed for the long-term transference of ideas and culture. Until the creation of Gutenberg's printing press, any book transcription was worth its weight in gold. These texts were painstakingly transcribed, page by page, from language to language, by dedicated scribes and scholars. Many of the sources for these transcriptions were Moorish works derived from texts originally written in Greek and Latin.

Transmission of knowledge from the Islamic world to

Europe is said to have originated in different places including Sicily and Toledo, Spain. These translations include the lost texts of Aristotle discovered by Burgundio of Pisa and translated into Latin. Many of these works not only found their way into European culture, but influenced European writings as well.

It was first suggested by Miguel Asín Palacios in 1919 that Dante Alighieri's Divine Comedy, considered the greatest epic of Italian literature, derived many features of and episodes about the hereafter directly or indirectly from Arabic works on Islamic eschatology, such as the Hadith and the spiritual writings of Ibn Arabi. The Kitab al-Miraj, concerning Muhammad's *'Ascension to Heaven',,* was translated into Latin circa 1264 as *'Liber Scale Machometi'*, "*The Book of Muhammad's Ladder*". Dante was certainly aware of Muslim philosophy, as he named Avicenna and Averroes in his list of non-Christian philosophers in Limbo, along with the great Greek and Latin philosophers. How strong the similarities are to Kitab al-Miraj remains a matter of scholarly debate however, with no clear evidence that Dante was in fact influenced.

Many Moorish works have been translated by many different cultures which include:

- An Arab manual of medical theory into Latin by Stefan of Pise around 1127;
- Leonardo Fibonacci's method of algorism developed by al-Khwarizmi in the 9th century to Europe by (1170–1250).

- A translation by Robert of Chester of al-Kharizmi's the Algebra;
- the compiled treatises on optical sciences by Ibn al-Haytham.

Many of the more sought-after texts such as the Almagest, had also been translated from Latin or Greek into Arabic. In a time where Europeans could barely read or write, Islamic Spain hosted many multi-lingual scholars and Arabic books on almost every subject which were subsequently translated from Arabic into Latin. This phenomenon contributed greatly to the growth and development of European sciences. Gerard of Cremona, noted European scholar personally translated many books from Arabic into Latin, including:

- the Almagest,
- the Book of Seventy,
- Muhammad ibn Mūsā al-Khwārizmī's On Algebra;
- Almucabala, Jabir ibn Aflah's Elementa astronomica;
- al-Kindi's On Optics,
- Ahmad ibn Muhammad ibn Kathīr al-Farghānī's On Elements of Astronomy on the Celestial Motions,
- al-Farabi's On the Classification of the Sciences
- the chemical and medical works of Rhazes
- the works of Thabit ibn Qurra and Hunayn ibn Ishaq,
- and the works of Arzachel, Jabir ibn Aflah, the

Banū Mūsā, Abū Kāmil Shujā ibn Aslam, Abu al-Qasim al-Zahrawi (Abulcasis), and Ibn al-Haytham (including the Book of Optics).

From Islamic Spain, the Arabic philosophical literature was translated into Hebrew, Latin, and Ladino. The Jewish philosopher Moses Maimonides, Muslim sociologist-historian Ibn Khaldun, Carthage citizen Constantine the African who translated Greek medical texts, and Al-Khwarizmi's collation of mathematical techniques were important figures of the Golden Age.

Logic

These 'Arabic' concepts of psychology and theory of knowledge particularly influenced two great Parisian minds in William of Auvergne and Albertus Magnus as well. However, the most influence in medieval Europe was due Averroes, another influential Muslim philosopher, whose concept of Aristotelianism disagreed with Avicenna's concept of Avicennism in the area of 'unity of the intellect' and 'existence precedes essence'. These concepts were key in shaping the religious frame that encased medieval Europe.

Avicennism and Averroism are terms for the revival of the Peripatetic school in medieval Europe due to the influence of Avicenna and Averroes, respectively. Averroes was influential in planting the seed of secular thought in Western Europe. Avicenna was noted for modifying the works of Aristotle with logic and original 'existence-essence' thinking relating to the nature of the 'soul'.

Sciences

The Arabic numerals, brought to Europe by Muslims (specifically the number zero (0), along with the decimal system), reduced their problem-solving to minutes instead of hours. These simple changes in the field of mathematics helped to lay the foundation for Europe's Scientific revolution.

Al Kawarizmi, one of the most popular Muslim mathematicians laid the ground work for algebra. He was called 'The Father of Algebra' because he also created ways to work with complex mathematical problems, including square roots and complex fractions. The proof of this can be found in Frederick Rosen's 1831 edition of Al-Khwarizmi's Algebra.

The 'scientific method' can also be attributed to the Muslims, specifically, Jabir ibn-Hayyan. The development of chemistry and alchemy in Europe can be traced back to this source. Even the terms alkali, elixir, alchohol and alembic are originally Islamic.
These scientific advances made during the Islamic Golden Age, in mathematics and astronomy (algebra, spherical trigonometry), and in chemistry, were also adopted by the West.

Alchemy

Western alchemy was directly impacted by Arabic sources including The Latin alchemical works of "Geber" (Jābir ibn Hayyān) These were in fact the standard texts for European alchemists. There is no doubting the influence on medieval European alchemy of the translated Arabic works.

The exact attribution of these works remains a matter of some controversy. Some are undoubtedly translations from Arabic from works attributed to Jābir ibn Hayyān, including the Kitab al-Kimya (titled Book of the Composition of Alchemy in Europe), translated by Robert of Chester (1144).

Astronomy, Mathematics and Physics

The translation of Al-Khwarizmi's work greatly influenced mathematics in Europe. His scientific work includes many different fields of interest including algebra, astronomy, astrology, geography and cartography. His experiments paved the way for principles we use today. Trigonometry was introduced and refined in northern Spain by Alkirmani of Toledo, after which it was translated into Latin. He also brought the Greek knowledge of Geometry by Euclid.
The study of Optics by Ibnul Hairhum were adopted as well, and even many of the principles or Sir Isaac Newton were guided by the Muslim Principle of Pendulum – which was used to measure time.

It is notable to say that much of plane and spherical trigonometry could be attributed to Islamic authors. The word algorithm comes from Al-Khwarizmi's Latinized name Algorismi, whereas the word algebra is said to have come from the title of his AD 820 book Hisab al-jabr w'al-muqabala.

Many other Arabic mathematical, as well as astronomical works were translated into Latin in the 12th century, including those by al-Battani, Muhammad al-Fazari and Brahmagupta and carried over to the Byzantine empire. Kitab al-Jabr wa-l-Muqabala are themselves Arabic loanwords.

Al-Khazini's Zij as-Sanjari (1115–1116) was translated into Greek by Gregory Choniades in the 13th century and was studied in the Byzantine Empire.

Al-Battani and Averroes modified the astronomical Ptolemaic model and led to other models by Mo'ayyeduddin Urdi, Nasīr al-Dīn al-Tūsī with Ibn al-Shatir, which were subsequently combined with the Copernican heliocentric model.

Abū al-Rayhān al-Bīrūnī's Ta'rikh al-Hind and Kitab al-qanun al-Mas'udi were translated into Latin as Indica and Canon Mas'udicus respectively. Liber Abaci is Fibonacci's presentation of the first complete account of Arabic numerals and the Hindu-Arabic numeral system to Europe.

Al-Jayyani's 'The Book of Unknown Arcs of a Sphere' (a treatise on spherical trigonometry) had a, or the, defining influence on European mathematics. Regiomantus' 'On Triangles' (1463) did in fact take much of his material on spherical trigonometry from the 12th-century work of Jabir ibn Aflah, as noted in the 16th century by Gerolamo Cardano.

The Book of Optics was one of the most important

advances of the scientific method of optics and its Latin translation greatly influenced almost all European scientists to follow, not excluding Roger Bacon and Johannes Kepler. Even Ptolemy's previous theory that light was emitted by the eye was challenged by Ibn al-Haytham in his Book of Optics which implied instead that light rays entered the eye, the most significant advance in this field until Kepler.

The book also made the connection between science and religion as Protestant Reformation intellectual John Wycliffe referred to it in his discussion about the seven deadly sins being compared to distortions in the seven types of mirrors from De Aspectibus. This book was also used in literature, art and even cartography.

Jean Buridan, who focused on logic, is said to have begun the Copernican revolution in Europe. He is credited for having developed the concept of impetus, the first step toward the modern concept of inertia and one of the most important developments in the history of medieval science. His concepts of inertia and momentum and his theory of impetus may have been influenced by the theory of motion by Avicenna from Aristotelian physics. Medieval physics writer Avempace also influenced the work of Galileo Galilei, superseding Aristotelian physics on classical mechanics. Even the magnetic compass, a Chinese invention, which revolutionized travel on land and sea, is first mentioned in Arabic sources by the Yemeni Sultan al-Ashraf, and, by Egyptian astronomer Ibn Sim'un as well.

On the Motions of the Heavens by Nur Ed-Din Al

Betrugi, Introduction to Astrology from Abu Mashar, Abū Kāmil Shujā ibn Aslam's Algebra, all had major impact on European culture and learning.

Agriculture and textiles

The Islamic Agricultural Revolution as it turns out was not well documented. It seems however that the seventh and eighth centuries sparked the spread of the Islamic agricultural system which had its source in India, the East and as far back as the Zingh Dynasty. Agriculture was shared by the Arabs primarily with those which they conquered as well as lands with whom they simply interacted. Unfriendly terrain and unstable climate oftentimes made the applications difficult, but centuries of know how prevailed. It is safe to say that the introduction of agriculture helped a starving Europe begin to not only feed itself, but add an economical viable industry as well.

Nutritious fruits and vegetables such as the aubergine, the artichoke and spinach, introduced to Europe in the Middle Ages sparked the economy, creating jobs and providing much needed sustenance. The introduction of water clocks, pulp and paper, the extraction of sugar from sugar cane and silk to Europe can also be attributed to the Islamic culture.

Arts

The Moorish, or Islamic influence also surfaced in the form of art and architecture throughout medieval Europe including mosaics and metal inlays, sculpture, and bronze-working. Islamic pottery, textiles and decorations adorned European churches and households. The high-quality textiles were preferred by the rich and affluent, as well as churches for shrouds, vestments, curtains and wall hangings. Ironically, most Christian households were adorned with Islamic art, as the scenery and language (usually Arabic and therefore, not understood anyway), were non obtrusive. The Norman, Arab and Byzantine influences in medieval art made their way across Europe, impacting concepts, perception and creativity.

Writing

In the area of writing, pseudo-Kufic, a copy of Arabic Kufic became the norm. Previously used for decoration, these angular and straight elements grace many Renaissance paintings and other forms of art in European culture. Many Westerners erroneously associated the Christian scripts current during Jesus's time with 13th and 14th-century Middle-Eastern scripts. Some say the church's ambition for international expansion drove the blending together of Islamic and Christian art.

The blending of these cultures was ever apparent in the carpets that graced the homes of the wealthy. These signs of luxury, typically depicting religious subjects, came from the Ottoman Empire, as well as the Levant and Egypt.

Music

Even European music and instruments were influenced by Arabic, as well as African music and musical instruments. These instruments include the rebec, the rebab, the qitara, the naqareh, the zamr, and the al-zuma. These became some of the violins and guitars we still use today.many of Europe's Medieval troubadours may have 'borrowed' from Arabic composers as well. William VIII after his experience with Moorish arts while fighting with the Reconquista in Spain was said to have been the originator of Europe's troubadour tradition. Certainly "a body of song of comparable intensity, profanity and eroticism [existed] in Arabic from the second half of the 9th century onwards."

Technology and culture

Technology was also introduced to Europe through the Moors. These innovations came in the forms of astronomical instruments (such as the astronomical sextant and the Quadrans Vetus), various surgical instruments and advanced gearing in waterclocks. The Arabs also introduced distillation and far too many other innovations to Europe that can be listed here.

Although disputed by Michael Decker, historian Andrew Watson postulated in 1974 that between the years 700-1100, there existed an Arab Agricultural Revolution bringing both technology and sustainable crops to medieval Europe, changing the culture, economy and labor force. Watson implies that crops from Africa, China and India changed the diet and thus the health and lifespan of those living in Europe during that time. He says that citrus fruits, rice, mangos, cotton, sugar cane, distributed throughout Islamic lands eventually found their way to European shores which improved population growth, income levels, agricultural production and urban growth.

Innovations such as the Mill and suction pumps are said to have also impacted the stagnant European culture as they automated tasks previously done with manual labor. Even European architecture is a blend of cultures. Arab-Norman art with Classical pillars, Islamic decorations and calligraphy, and other Occidental features adorned halls, cathedrals and dwellings of the affluent.

There is no doubt that the Moors and their influence changed the culture of Europe and thereby, the entire civilized world. The question then becomes not whether or not the Moors contributed to the European culture through the European Renaissance, and thereby influencing modern America, the question becomes why is it important to hide the contributions?

CHAPTER 5

THE

REVOLUTIONARY WAR

the American colonists-particularly Southern colonists-were afraid that the British government would abolish slavery.

5 THE REVOLUTIONARY WAR

The Revolutionary War

America is a living mosaic of people, cultures, traditions and histories. These all combine to give her the unique character she possesses. The events that transpired on her soil and abroad, in the order they occurred, shaped the America we see today.

It was the agreements, as well as the disagreements that created this social and political structure we now enjoy, tolerate – or oppose. None of these disagreements were as important to the development of the land than the Revolutionary War. Today's America began as settlements and colonies, and, there were varying opinions on how she should be developed.

Having been settled by the Dutch, British, Spanish and the French, this new frontier presented opportunities for discovery, growth and advancement, for each of these countries. Each country had its own set of traditions, culture, rules and regulations, which they imposed on their respective colonists. Nonetheless, the opportunities afforded by this rich land made its colonization well worth the effort and investment. At the forefront of these new opportunities stood Great Britain who had already established colonies all over the world.

In the early 1700's, the new-world colonists sought to become independent of British government rule and the accompanying taxation. This "Taxation without representation", along with the fact that the colonists had no voice in the British Parliament didn't help that relationship at all. To be clear, another main cause for this Revolutionary War was the colonists wanting to print their own money. This is logical in that they could then set the value of their currency and charge what they wanted in interest without oversight.

Before the war, the colonies sent Benjamin Franklin to England to represent their interests. Franklin was greatly surprised by the amount of poverty and high unemployment. It just didn't make sense, England was the richest country in the world but the working class was impoverished, he wrote *"The streets are covered with beggars and tramps."*
This may not be treated as a casual phenomenon as basic statistical analyses apply.

It's All About the Money

Circa 1750, the English bankers demanded that the King and Parliament pass a law that prevented the colonists from using their own land-backed money. These English bankers proposed that only money backed by gold and silver provided by them should be recognized as legal tender. The laws passed by Britain in 1751, and then 1763 created debt-based money that would send the American economy and its working class into a continued downward spiral as the supply of money had been cut in half.

The British currency which was forced on the colonists was supposed to have been based on the gold and silver standard, but since there were insufficient reserves to back it, the currency devalued quickly. At the time when the colonists began their revolt, Congress issued 'Continental Dollars' to support the war, which, like the British currency, were supposed to have been backed by gold and silver. Like today, those gold and silver reserves didn't exist, so the government's promise to redeem those dollars were not taken seriously – which also devalued that currency. Further depreciation and devaluation occurred when England printed large amounts of counterfeit Continental Dollars and flooded the colonies with it. This depreciation caused mass unemployment and created beggars which, as Benjamin Franklin stated on the previous visit to parliament, didn't exist in the colonies. In 1781, in a subsequent booklet entitled "*Of the Paper Money of America*", Franklin writes that the depreciation of the Continental dollar behaved as an inflation tax and as such, fell more equally across citizenry than most other taxes. At that time, it was the general consensus that war and or plagues were necessary to slow the population and rid the land of manpower surpluses.

The taxes were presumably unfairly levied because the colonists had no representation in the British Parliament, so it began to feel like slavery. Sovereignty or self-government and financial independence were key to lasting freedoms, according to our Founding Fathers, and, our ignorance of money matters facilitated their end.

Another of the driving forces behind the Revolutionary War was the desire of rich land owners to get richer, while paying out as little as possible. In the colonies, especially the south, slavery was the oil that fueled their economy. Slavery created the social and economic environment protected and lauded by the Southern governments and its leaders. Slavery in the southern colonies made white slave owners the wealthiest group on the mainland. These guys were making money hand over fist, as they, through slave labor, were harvesting crops with incredibly high yields. Add that to the fact that they were selling their cotton to Spain, Great Britain and Germany at discounted rates because of the extremely low overhead and it's easy to understand why they would resist taxation. How ironic that the people who didn't want to be treated like slaves, made much of their profits on slave labor.

So, the main reason for this war was money, though honor may have played an important role as well. What we have to remember is that England demanded at least three things from the colonists:

- the tribute or taxes;
- that the colonists use British currency; and,
- that the British colonies must abolish slavery.

The colonists in America who were land-owners found these demands unacceptable because all three directly impacted their bottom line. So, if the known cause of the Revolutionary war was taxation without representation, and the equally important cause was who's currency would be used, then the hidden and forgotten cause was definitely the issue of slavery. Add to that the stockpiling of guns and ammunition, and you have a recipe for war, or at the least, a confrontation. This combination of factors actually led to the first shots being fired at Lexington and Concord, starting the Revolutionary War.

A Change in Britain

During this time, approximately 100 years before the Emancipation Proclamation, in June (22) of 1772, the decision of a British Judge would impact slavery in the Colonies and subsequently, the United States - from the Revolutionary and Civil wars, until today. His decision to prohibit slavery in Britain would have profound economic and political effects in the founding of America as well as around the world as presented in the book – *'Slave Nation: How Slavery United the Colonies and Sparked the American Revolution'* by Alfred and Ruth Blumrosen. This book illustrates the fact that one of the main reasons for the Revolutionary War was the protection of slavery.

American economics and politics comprise a compendium of facts as they relate to our relationship with the privately controlled Bank of England, beginning prior to the Revolutionary war. In 1729, Benjamin Franklin, 'the father of America's paper money' wrote *"A Modest Enquiry into the Nature and Necessity of a Paper Currency"*. This booklet championed Pennsylvania's then well-known 'Paper Money Bill' which the common man saw as necessary and the rich saw as a liability. He, Ben Franklin reported that the country was stable and prosperous and that education and morality were the order of the day.

Franklin's book also addressed South Carolina's depreciating paper currency and offered a system that seemed to function in Pennsylvania and Massachusetts. He says that paper cures the ills of 'barter' the heir apparent through trade, to having shipped gold and silver back to England. His book stated that barter increased the cost of local exchange while lowering wages, employment and reducing immigration. He also wrote that paper money would reduce high local interest rates and increase investment – therefore speeding up development. He postulates that the quantity of paper money, relative to the volume of internal trade within the colonies is what controls the paper money's value. He also says the depreciation of paper money is caused by its excess relative to the volume of internal trade, not legal tender laws or fixed exchange rates. The same can be seen today.

He argues that paper money backed by gold and silver had no permanent value because the over-mining of these minerals made their value unstable. He proposes that instead of England's gold and silver backed paper monies, his offer would be to back Pennsylvania's paper money with land, as land holds its value and appreciates. This new paper money would be issued as loans and the land would be held as collateral.

All of these considerations combined to make southern political lawyers anxious about their property in slaves that was threatened by the Somerset decision. Taxation might have taken some of their property; Somerset threatened to take it all.

Franklin's book goes on to tell how major decisions made by the Americans - such as the agreement to break from British rule, the wording of the Declaration of Independence, and the formulation of the Articles of Confederation, as well as the Constitution-were all done in a manner that protected the right of the South to maintain slavery.

For example: in early drafts of the Declaration of Independence, the language that said "All men are born equally free and independent" was changed by Thomas Jefferson to "All men were created equal" to prevent the implication that slaves should be free. In the end, though, the Revolutionary War did not prevent the conflict over slavery from coming to a head; it merely delayed it.

As the book notes, many in the North (and some Southerners, too) abhorred slavery, but compromises were made continually with the Southerners for the sake of unity. While much of the enmity toward slavery was based on religious and moral grounds, some of it was based on economics. Many felt that slavery undercut the labor market for white men. Over time, anti-slavery sentiment grew to a boil.

However, most whites owned one or two slaves, not the much larger numbers owned by the major planters. But the feeling was that these few slaves were crucial to their masters in easing the daily labor necessary for to work farms, ranches and plantations. an agricultural existence. For example, owning slaves enabled white children to have some schooling, or enabled ill or disabled family members to bear lighter loads. The ironic part of this situation is that the work subsequently done by slaves was previously performed by a mixed population of poor whites and blacks – many of who were indentured servants. In 1676, those poor whites rebelled causing Virginia to shift its labor force to black, slave labor.

The South Rises

Here's the problem with the way the Revolutionary War is taught: much of the story about the War centers on the northern colonies, particularly Massachusetts, where pivotal events such as the Boston Tea Party and the Boston Massacre took place, and where the term "no taxation without representation" originated. And there's no doubt that Massachusetts was a flashpoint in the coming war of independence.

However, in the various congresses/meetings held by the colonies/states in the 1770s-1780s, it was the representatives from the South who were the primary, vocal and pressing in the advocacy of slavery (or more correctly, the states' right to allow slavery). Or at least: this is what is indicated by the historical record. This passage concerning comments from John Adams is an example. Adams made it clear in later life that he deferred to the Southerners on the issue of slavery: *"I constantly said in former times to the southern gentlemen, I cannot comprehend this object (slavery). I will vote for forcing no measure against your judgments."* This is NOT to say that at NO TIME did northern voices advocate for "slavery rights." But the record is clear (at least in this book) that the issue was pressed mainly/overwhelmingly by the southern states. The main point is that the American colonists-particularly Southern colonists-were afraid that the British government would abolish slavery. And that this fear was a major reason for the colonists' desire to break away from Great Britain., but there were 13 original colonies, and the southern colonies had a unique interest of their own to worry about: protecting their "right" to keep slaves. The landed white gentry of this country had no desire to share their wealth.

The Somerset Decision

The British courts decision that helped shape America would be initiated by abolitionists and others believing in equality. The 'Somerset Case', decided in Britain in 1772, involving then slave James Somerset, was to shape America's politics, social system and economics for decades to come. The decision from this case would guide the wording of the Declaration of Independence, the Articles of the Confederation and the Constitution as well. Somerset, the property of Boston Massachusetts customs officer Charles Stewart, accompanied Stewart to England from America in 1769.. In late 1771, Somerset, witnessing the free Black community there, decided to escape and was eventually caught. Since at this time in England, slavery had been abolished, he was to have been sent to the British colonies in Jamaica. The lawyers and abolitionists who defended Somerset argued that ..."Even though slavery and other laws might be allowed in the colonies, neither the common law of England nor any law made by Parliament recognized the existence of slavery, and therefore, slavery was illegal". Lord Mansfield, the Chief Justice of the King's Bench, said in his ruling:

"The state of slavery is of such a nature, that it is incapable of being introduced on any reasons, moral or political; but only positive law, which preserves its force long after the reasons, occasion, and time itself from whence it was created, is erased from memory: it's so odious, that nothing can be suffered to support it, but positive law. Whatever inconveniences, therefore, may follow from a decision, I cannot say this case is allowed or approved by the law of England; and therefore the black must be discharged. "

News of this verdict must have put fear in the hearts, and sent shivers up the spines of most slave owners because the charters from Britain contained "repugnancy clauses" which prohibited Americans from creating legislation contrary to British laws. In fact, in 1766 the British passed the Declaratory Act giving the British parliament jurisdiction over all cases whatsoever involving American laws. What that meant was if Britain were to make America an extension of the commonwealth, the South would lose its principle source of income. The culture of slavery also represented an economic and social environment protected by the leaders of the day. The Somerset Case actually caused many southern land-owners to literally hate the British for this decision that promised to eventually send them to the poorhouse.

In addition, there was the concern that the American slaves would hear about the decision and also want to escape to England where, due to the decision, they too would be free. This was important as the slaves themselves represented at least four sources of income: as collateral and security for loans, the high productivity yields, the slaves reproducing more slaves and the value of the land they cleared and replanted over and over again.

A BLACK THREAD

CHAPTER 6

THE CIVIL WAR

The amount of money assembled from a dictatorship is the amount needed to insure that dictatorship stays in power

6 THE CIVIL WAR

What actually caused the Civil War?

Of course we all know that slavery wasn't the only reason for the Civil war, but it ranks in the top two. If it wasn't slavery, then it was definitely what slavery brought – extreme wealth, with little overhead. Land ownership with a regenerating labor force, and, the products that labor force produced.

The South profited from slave labor while the North built and perfected their factories. This mechanization of tasks allowed less-skilled workers to permeate that marketplace. The point is that rich Southern land owners growing sugar cane, cotton, tobacco, and soy beans had little to no overhead. These crops didn't need to be manufactured or assembled, only harvested, cleaned and delivered. But, who is that doing the picking, cutting, cleaning, bailing, carrying and re-planting. Who is that working from sun-up, until sundown, or as they used to say in the South "From cain't to cain't"? That means it's dark so you can't see when you begin working, and dark when you finish. It was the slaves, share-croppers and indentured servants who toiled in sun-baked fields, day in and day out. That is the beauty of the Southern system – no wages, proper food or even proper lodging was provided those who produced the products that made millions for these people.

The amount of money assembled from a dictatorship is the amount needed to insure that dictatorship stays in power. The amount of money made from slave labor and sale of slave-produced products was obscene, even by today's standards. That faction would control media outlets, military and key strategic geographical locations for a long, long time and still does today. That is why the founding White gentry of America stays in power, because it takes a substantial amount of money to control information and fuel the campaigns that win elections.

This quote says it all:

"This could not be more true than with Donald Trump: a white man who would not be president - were he not white. In fact, except for Obama, many of those who held the position did so through blood-power, or "the passive power of whiteness" (Which, is evidenced by many of our former presidents being father and son). Though many of our former leaders did not possess the knowledge required to hold the offices for which they were chosen, they fit the right profile. Treachery, cunning, exclusion and lies facilitated the land theft and human plunder that opened the floodgates of prosperity for our founding forefathers. These ethics were also the basis for the documents that would prevent others the same opportunities. These sins, having seemingly been forgotten, are still the basis for the laws and mandates that govern almost the entire world. The bloodstained soil upon which we stand will forever echo the triumphs and losses of the winners and losers that fought upon her.

From the wilderness to the White House they cleared a

path through whoever, or whatever may have stood in their way. So, the inheritance left to Donald Trump and those of his ilk bears a hefty price – costing much more that the riches acquired from those questionable victories."

The Slavery Machine

Let's be perfectly clear, when we talk about slavery, we are talking about the subjugation, torture, humiliation, division, and murder of individuals and families. These tactics are necessary in order to establish control and dominance over the subjected. The costs however, are immeasurable, as what these who are subjected to this treatment can never see or reach is their full potential. While this serves to maintain the status quo, it severely impacts society as it hinders the creativity and all but kills the advancements these people could contribute to that society. Slavery was to become one of the main factors which decided the structure as well as the geographical layout of America. The Missouri Compromise ensured the balance of slave-holding and free states, but ordinances like the 'Fugitive Slave Act' ensured that all states participated in the system of slavery.

The slavery machine would find support on the highest levels as In 1857, as part of the Dred Scott ruling, the Supreme Court ruled that Congress had no right to prohibit slavery in territories. Pulitzer Prize-winning author James McPherson said it best:

"The Civil War started because of uncompromising differences between the free and slave states over the

power of the national government to prohibit slavery in the territories that had not yet become states. When Abraham Lincoln won election in 1860 as the first Republican president on a platform pledging to keep slavery out of the territories, seven slave states in the Deep South seceded and formed a new nation, the Confederate States of America. The incoming Lincoln administration and most of the Northern people refused to recognize the legitimacy of secession. They feared that it would discredit democracy and create a fatal precedent that would eventually fragment the no-longer United States into several small, squabbling countries. "

There were about 22million people in the North and 9 million in the south. The sentiment of individual states was echoed in one of the strangest presidential elections in American history.

Politics and Slavery

The election of 1860 played more than an important part in the Civil War. Since the North and South were divided, there were representatives from various parties including Abraham Lincoln of Illinois, Republican Party; Stephen A. Douglas of Illinois, Northern Democratic Party:; John C. Breckenridge of Kentucky, Southern Democratic Party; and John Bell of Tennessee, Constitutional Union Party. If you want to get a sense of what this was like, imagine two trumps, a Hillary and an Obama.

What would have happened if Breckenridge or Bell had won the election of 1860? Bell won the key slave

states of Virginia, Tennessee and Kentucky and since Lincoln wasn't even on most Southern ballots, Breckenridge won the other Southern States. Douglas only took electoral votes from Missouri and New Jersey. The issue that decided the outcome of this election was slavery.
Choosing Sides

As to the question 'Was secession legal?', the answer lies in Chief Justice Salmon Chase's majority opinion in *Texas v's White*. Although it was not ruled illegal until after the war, Texas v's White determined that secession was unconstitutional. Chief Justice Chase wrote: that, *"The ordinance of secession...and all the acts of legislature intended to give effect to that ordinance, were absolutely null. They were utterly without operation in law."*

The battles of the Civil War were fought in many, many different places including the Gulf of Mexico, the Mississippi River and the Atlantic Ocean as far away as the coast of France. Most of the fighting, however, was done in the states of Virginia and Tennessee.

The number of people who fought for each side includes 2,128,948 for the North, and the number for the South was 1,082,119, according to sources. The initial number of the dead was said to have been 620,000, but that figure has recently been updated at 850,000. My question, do those figures accurately reflect the Blacks who fought and died for each side? In any event, these deaths are attributed to combat, accidents and starvation.

Here is a chronological list of the states that seceded from the Union: South Carolina - December 20, 1860; Mississippi - January 9, 1861; Florida - January 10, 1861; Alabama - January 11, 1861; Georgia - January 19, 1861; Louisiana - January 26, 1861; Texas - February 1, 1861; Virginia - April 17, 1861; Arkansas - May 6, 1861; North Carolina - May 20, 1861; Tennessee - June 8, 1861.

To understand how much conviction fueled this war, one has to compare the body-count of this horrific encounter to other wars in which America was involved. Approximately 850k died in this war while WWII, WWI, Vietnam and Korea host 405.4k, 116.5k, 58.2k and 36.5k, respectively.

What could divide friends and family, states and nations? What could possibly make one look at a family member and say "This is more important to me than your very life!". The issue of slavery not only divided families, it also heightened the awareness of State's rights.

States' Rights in the Colonies

What do we mean by States' Rights? States' Rights is a term used to describe the ongoing struggle over political power in the United States between the Federal Government and individual states as broadly outlined in the Tenth Amendment of the Constitution and whether the USA is a single entity or an amalgamation of independent nations. In modern times the term States Rights has also come to symbolize the opposition of some states to federal mandated laws against racial segregation and discrimination.

Even as far back as 1776, following separation from Great Britain, each state saw themselves as a sovereign, or independent territory. The pains of the Revolutionary War created the need for a central government, out of which came the Articles of Confederation. This was an agreement created by the Continental Congress that was to have established the much needed Central Government, but failed as the individual states went about the business of creating their own laws. It was like having rebellious children living under one roof, each attempting to run the household as he or she saw fit, with each jurisdiction changing from room to room, often while ignoring the house rules.

Constitutional Divide

With all its seemingly perfect parts and well thought-out construction, whose initial thrust was to form a more perfect union which included freedoms of speech, religion, assembly, the right to bear arms, the United States Constitution greatly strengthened the Central Government. Through the establishment of this more perfect union, states could now share taxes, share militia when needed, and take advantage of a relatively equal, mutually beneficial system of government.
However, this great document that has run America since 1789, was severely flawed. For a document that

was written to address federal, state's and individual rights for ALL Americans, it seemed a tad askew. What was added and what was left out clearly favored the founding white gentry and their families, holding sway over the poor and minorities. Prior to the amendments, the phrase "by the people" or "for the people" written in the Constitution didn't include 'All' people as illustrated by the Ninth Amendment which stated, "The enumeration in the Constitution of certain rights shall not be construed to deny or disparage others retained by the people,". It is imperative to note that as this was being written, the majority of those who drafted it were slave owners. One of the main loopholes in the Constitution to allow for the maintenance of slavery was/is the Tenth Amendment which leaves that door wide open by stating:

"The powers not delegated to the United States by the Constitution, nor prohibited by it to the States, are reserved to the States respectively, or to the people."

These are two of the most important amendments to slaveholding states because it allowed them the authority to continue the practice of slavery with impunity. This privilege did much to separate the states as many states had their own agendas, many of which disagreed with some of the mandates found within this new Constitution. A few of the northern states thrived on industry the products of which were traded with Britain, as well as with other European countries.

Many of the Southern states were offended that Britain wanted to control the colonies because under British rule, slavery was prohibited and they wanted no one tampering with their money machine. The sentiment of these slave states saw no end, as their focus and policies continued to strengthen the slavery platform.

This dispute affected many states in various ways. For example, during the War of 1812, the liberal New England states sought to secede from the union in order to continue trading with Britain. Many of the Southern states were offended that Britain wanted to abolish slavery, and didn't love that , as previously stated, under British rule, slavery was prohibited in its colonies. The exports of these New England states were a significant portion of their economy and many of them were also against the practice of slavery.

Here's where it gets confusing to me. The Northern manufacturing states had more overhead and costs, yet it was the Southern slave-holding states, particularly South Carolina, who opposed the tariffs imposed by the federal government. This sentiment led to the 'Nullification Crisis' wherein South Carolina deemed the tariffs imposed by the federal government unconstitutional and therefore, 'null and void'. Although the 'Compromise Tariff of 1833' seemed to temporarily quell the dispute, this disagreement, among other factors, eventually led to South Carolina's secession from the Union.

The divide over slavery wasn't just political and economic, it was also geographical. The states below the 'Mason-Dixon Line' used slave labor to cultivate cotton, tobacco and sugar cane crops. These three were of the most sought after of the time and their harvesting resulted in the landowners' then unfathomable riches. And, since nepotism and cronyism were the order of the day, they were sure to stay in power. So, in effect, states' rights had more to do with money than politics. Let's bring it into perspective.

Dollars and Sense

Imagine one neighborhood with two sides of the same street. On one side, 'Side A', are people who manufacture widgets. On the other side , 'Side B', are those who farm land using horses to plow fields of regenerative crops like potatoes. Those on side A pay their employees and taxes, pay for raw materials, R&D, processing, packaging, rent and delivery. Those on side B pay for the horses and the plows. The horses will regenerate so the investment in raw materials is only an initial, one-time investment. They do not feed them, but provide them water and scraps. They are beaten and forced to work from morning until night. There are no costs for salaries and only a one-time cost for raw materials. So, with minimal investment and minimal effort, model B reaps mega rewards.

Retaining a percentage of a percentage of a percentage from the costs of doing business is a far cry from only having to pay taxes and transport, shipping and delivery. The percentages to which I'm referring include but are not necessarily limited to: taxes, salaries and bonuses, insurance, paid leave and vacations, security, raw materials, manufacturing and processing, research and development, transport, shipping and delivery, and far too many others to mention here.

When President Thomas Jefferson purchased 828,000 acres of heartland from Napoleon of France for a little more than $11 million in 1803, his purchase raised the question: Should the states created out of that land be slave or free?

Louisiana had been carved out and accepted as a slave state in 1812, but no other territory had petitioned Congress for statehood out of the purchase lands until Missouri did so in 1818, also wanting to enter the Union as a slave state. That request threatened to unsettle a delicate balance of 11 slave and 11 free states, a balance both sides found necessary for maintaining equal representation in the Senate.

In 1819, the representative from New York, James Tallmadge proposed the Tallmadge Amendment, which addressed the issue of slaves in Missouri and advocated for their emancipation. It is no surprise that at the time, Southern states vehemently protested the Tallmadge Amendment, claiming that if it forced Missouri to enter the Union as a free state, it would upset the existing free-state, slave-state balance, giving the free-states unfair advantage and therefore, a political edge.

What it eventually came down to was plantation economy vs. the farm-and-industry economic model. So, even though the Northern state's representatives saw the slaves as little more than property, slavery posed a major threat to their industrial economic model. They also wanted to keep land otherwise designated for plantations, for farmers and their families.

Slavery – A Legal Entity

It is important to remember that initially, slavery was legal, and therefore found in all states. In order to have the Constitution ratified by all states, they made sure to avoid the specific mention of slavery. However, the writers of the Constitution, most of whom possessed slaves, made sure that the Constitution protected their interests. For example, the provision that made a fugitive from one state a fugitive in every state made certain that a run-away slave in a free state was still, by law, legally a slave. This, more than anything else, began to shed light on the inconsistency of state's rights. Abolitionists from the North began to fight the institution of slavery and the states that practiced it - aiding in the escapes of run-away slaves. The existence of slavery in most states below the Mason-Dixon Line compelled many Northern Abolitionists to use force, often assaulting slave owners and hunters of run-away slaves.

The expansion of the US territory to the Pacific Ocean as a result of the victory in the Mexican war raised further questions about whether or not to permit slavery in these new territories. This intense discussion widened the chasm between slave-holding and free states which finally erupted with the establishment of the new, regional Republican Party, and, ensuing election of its candidate, Abraham Lincoln. Since Abraham Lincoln opposed slavery, his election caused the slave-holding states to secede from the Union.

The question of federal vs. state power was illuminated by the descriptions of the country as "The United States are" before the Civil War and "The United States is" after. Similar to the aftermath of the establishment of the subsequent Berlin Wall, the country was divided, separating families and cities, as well as states. For example, Virginia lost counties to the seceding state of West Virginia and even lost the suit to reclaim them.

States' Rights & the Civil War

In a nutshell, 'States' rights' came down to who was allowed, per the Constitution, to keep slaves. The struggle between the federal government and individual states over political power would determine the course America would eventually take. The fact that a slave was constitutionally seen as property, and therefore, three-fifths of a man shouted at least two glaring weaknesses in the system as devaluing a human is barbaric, and, just like today, the black vote would prove more valuable than originally forecasted. This is something they obviously knew about the power of the black vote during the establishment of the separate, but united, states. This dichotomy that existed inside itself was fueled by the economics of slave labor.

The election of Abraham Lincoln of the new

Republican Party in 1859, a powerful opponent of the expansion of slavery, was the straw that broke the camel's back! The Southern states seceded from the Union.

1925, Gitlow vs. New York, in keeping with the 14th Amendment, said that the Bill of Rights applies to the states - and the Federal Government. In 1820, the proposal suggested by Illinois Senator Jesse B. Thomas, said that Maine would enter as a free state and Missouri could enter with slaves. In addition, no slavery would be permitted north in states out of the Louisiana Purchase - north of 36 degrees 30 minutes latitude or Missouri's southern boundary. This proposal was accepted in the Senate but defeated in the House, increasing the slavery debate in Congress. After a time and much deliberation, both the North and South accepted Thomas' compromise as a resolution to the problem, finally agreeing upon what would be called the 'Missouri Compromise'.

The Missouri Compromise:

Missouri Applies For Statehood

Once again, Slavery proved to be an issue that divided the nation. Yes, slavery, indirectly economics, decided how the nation would be divided and Missouri was one of the main catalysts. Even though the Northwest Ordinance of 1787 prohibited slavery in much of the north, many of the Southerners migrating to the north took slaves with them disguised as then legal, indentured servants. These Southerners even defended and tried to justify their "peculiar institution," while Northerners postulated that "slave power" was taking all the land. The fear was that this trend would spread throughout the north and when states like Missouri were admitted, it would add to the expansion of slavery in the northern regions.

Many abolitionists, including Congressman Arthur Livermore of New Hampshire wondered "how long will the desire for wealth render us blind to the sin of holding our fellow men in chains?"
In 1819, this slaveholding territory of Missouri applied for admission to the Union. Northern states opposed it, feeling that Southern slaveholding states held too much political power already. The Constitution allowed states to count each slave as three-fifths of a person for purposes of determining population, and therefore, the number of Congressional representatives to which that state was entitled. This had given the South an advantage in Congress.

Missouri's application for statehood brought with it controversy as it, a slave state, would most certainly upset the balance of the already unstable Union. Due to the unfair Constitutional three-fifths voting representation, the Northern states opposed Missouri's application as the South already had a political advantage. The Missouri Compromise of 1820 set the practice of admitting states into the Union in pairs, one free state, and one slave state. For example, Missouri and Maine were admitted as a pair. This compromise had many significant elements, two of the most significant being the aforementioned prohibition of slavery above parallel 36 degrees, 30 minutes within the lands of the Louisiana Purchase, and, the national Fugitive Slave Law, which mandated that all Americans return runaway slaves to their owners.

The Missouri Compromise appeared to be a solution to the slavery crisis up until the Mexican War in 1846. However, the outcome of this war brought more land under the United States' control, which again, fanned the flames of the slavery controversy.

The Abolitionist Movement

It is written in American history that African slavery began in America in the year 1619 at Jamestown, Virginia. Ironically, these same slaves were forced to help build the first American-built slave ship, Desire, which was launched from Massachusetts, beginning the slave trade between Africa and Britain's American colonies., The first mention of the American-built slave ship was in John Winthrop's journal, according to the Massachusetts Historical Society. Following the Pequot War of 1637, it transported captive Pequot Indians to the West Indies in exchange for African slaves, initiating the intercontinental slave trade.

The year 1859 saw two events that were milestones in the history of slavery and abolition in America. The ship Clotilde landed in Mobile, Alabama. Though the importation of slaves had been illegal in America since 1808, Clotilde carried 110 to 160 African slaves. The last slave ship ever to land in the United States, it clearly demonstrated how lax the enforcement of the slavery anti-importation laws was.

The noble Abolitionist movement in the United States of America was intended to end slavery in a nation that preached personal freedom values believing "all men are created equal." Even though, beginning in 1808, the Constitution prohibited importation of slaves, many states managed to do so without using the words "slave" or "slavery." To note, slave trading became a capital offense in 1819. History reveals that it was not just "taxation without representation" that led to the American Revolution (as mentioned in the previous chapter), and the American Civil War, but also division over abolitionists and slave-holding states over the right to keep slaves.

Keep in mind, the South not only did not want to abolish slavery, they wanted it to last forever. That means they had, and would continue to set up provision for their descendants to continue in this fashion. When we look at the need for a Civil Rights Bill, then we see the system of inequality mapped out by this founding gentry to keep their offspring large and in charge.

However, many white colonists were uncomfortable with the notion of slavery from the beginning. During the American Revolution against the English Crown, Delaware and Virginia prohibited importation of African slaves. In 1777, Vermont was the first of the 13 colonies to abolish slavery and a year later, Rhode Island banned taking slaves from the colony while Pennsylvania began a form of emancipation in 1780. They also had to prove that one person owning another was morally wrong, so first they had to convince many, all over the country, that Negroes, the term used for the race at the time, were human. Even with all of the evidence, many of these abolitionists also believed that blacks were not equal to whites.

1789 marked the founding of the Maryland Society for Promoting the Abolition of Slavery and the Relief of Free Negroes and Others Unlawfully Held in Bondage. This was the same year "in order to form a more perfect union", the former colonies replaced their Articles of Confederation with the new Constitution. Even though the original U.S. Constitution was written without specific, mention of slavery, it made provisions for the return of 'fugitives' (meaning criminals, slaves and indentured servants). Because Article I, Section 3, of the Constitution says "representation and direct taxation will be determined based on the number of 'free persons', including those bound to service for a term of years, and excluding Indians not taxed, three-fifths of all other persons", the Constitution also allowed each slave within a state to be counted as three-fifths of a person for the purpose of determining population and representation in the House of Representatives.

The need for slavery seemed to grow as technology increased. With the invention of the cotton gin and sewing machine, the possibility and need for increased production of cotton made slavery even more necessary. The shift from, "Slavery is a necessary evil," to "Slavery is a positive good" was the consensus of the Southern states during the 1830's. It was widely believed and postulated that the institution of slavery existed because it was "God's will," a Christian duty to lift the African out of barbarism while still exerting control over his "animal passions." The anti-black, racist activity and mindset we saw take the life of an anti-racist woman in Charlotte, SC, began long before 2017. The first American Anti-Slavery Society Convention in 1833 in Philadelphia ended in anti-abolition riots in New York, Philadelphia and many other northeastern cities in the years following. The Carolinas petitioned other states to suppress human rights rhetoric from abolition groups. The many participants in the evolution of the fight for the abolishment of slavery have varying backgrounds, as well as reasons for their individual, and collective participation. We will list some of the most famous here. It is not to say that the contributions of the unknowns were any less significant, but we will direct our focus on the ones we know.

The many abolitionist that perpetuated change whom we know include: *Harriett Tubman; Sojourner Truth; John Brown; and Frederick Douglas*, to name a few.

The Kansas-Nebraska Act of 1854 allowed the citizens of those territories to determine for themselves whether the state would be slave or free. Proponents of both factions poured into the Kansas Territory, with each side trying to gain supremacy, often through violence. After pro-slavery groups attacked the town of Lawrence in 1856, a radical abolitionist named John Brown led his followers in retaliation, killing five pro-slavery settlers. The territory became known as "Bleeding Kansas."

Being caught in a slave state while aiding runaways was much more dangerous than in the North; punishments included prison, whipping, or even hanging—assuming that the accused made it to court alive instead of perishing at the hands of an outraged mob. White men caught helping slaves to escape received harsher punishments than white women, but both could expect jail time at the very least. The harshest punishments—dozens of lashes with a whip, burning or hanging—were reserved for any blacks caught in the act of aiding fugitives.

It was easy to treat these slaves as subhuman by forcing that distinction on them. By giving them names like 'Nigger', 'beasts' and 'chattel', and regarding them as animals, it was not necessary to treat them as human. So, beating them, working them excessively, starving them, and even killing them was, in the masters' eyes, legally, and morally, Ok. They found that, like an animal, the inherently rebellious slave had to be broken. They devised methods, much like what we see today in the news and on social media, to display the extreme punishment exacted upon the non-conformists in the forms of incarceration, beatings, and brutal death. They divided the normally strong family nucleus and sparked dissension among the groups by elevating certain among the slave ranks to places of pseudo-authority, thereby creating a buffer between themselves and this potentially volatile segment. Master's orders were sent via these proxies but punishment was meted out by the white overseers, keeping the balance while putting a black, or semi-black face on their immediate oppressor.

Abolitionists began to be more aggressive and visually active in condemning slave owners and what they called "the peculiar institution of slavery." Based on the language written in the constitution, abolitionists often used the 4th of July to denounce the document as what they called a "covenant with death, and an agreement with hell." A larger number of them started to believe in a "higher law". They believed that there was a moral commitment to ending slavery, and that this morality took precedent over the parts of the Constitution that protected both slavery and the Fugitive Slave Act.

Bounty-hunters and slave owners retrieving runaway slaves, in accordance with the Fugitive Slave Act, were often met with physical violence from abolitionist mobs. Even the local constabulary were not immune to these attacks. As pointed out by the Southern politicians of the day, who wanted slavery to continue, the South was required to obey all the laws, especially those pertaining to slavery and the expansion of slavery, but the Northerners could 'pick and choose' the laws they wanted to obey – further substantiating the secession argument.

Anti-Slavery Publications

Many New England families that had become wealthy through the slave trade well before restrictions against importing slaves were enforced, became abolitionists.

These abolitionists began to fight and speak out against slavery, through action, newspapers and pamphlets. By 1820, there were so many different of these publications that South Carolina instituted stiff penalties against those bringing anti-slavery material into the state.

Most of the above-mentioned anti-slavery publications presented slavery as a social and moral evil. They even presented examples of African American writings and other achievements to demonstrate that Africans and their descendants were not the animals they were portrayed to be. They were actually as capable of learning as were Europeans when given the freedom to do so.

One such publication was The Liberator, founded by William Lloyd Garrison in 1831. This is the same year of the Southampton Slave Riot also known as Nat Turner's Rebellion, which prompted Virginia to pass new regulations against slaves.

"It is no more harm for you to kill a man who is trying to kill you, than it is for you to take a drink of water when thirsty."

These are the words of David Walker, a freeman of color living in Boston, Massachusetts, in his publication, *"An Appeal to the Colored Citizens of the World"*. Originally from the South, he called for slaves to defend themselves, to rise up against their masters, and, prompted abolitionists to use more militant tactics.. As early as 1800, a Virginia slave known as Gabriel Prosser had attempted an uprising there, but it failed when two slaves betrayed his plan to their masters. Walker's publication, however was too extreme for even the most staunch abolition leaders, who feared the outcome of such tactics, as many were not prepared to kill or die for their beliefs.

Politics and the Election of Abraham Lincoln

The abolition movement was spurred by the aggregation of the Native American Party (the 'Know-Nothing Party), the Free Soil Party and many Whigs which In 1856 formed the Republican Party which, was responsible for the election of Abraham Lincoln in 1860.

When Abraham Lincoln, a member of the then anti-slavery Republican Party was elected in 1860, he mandated that the new territories acquired by the US would not allow the expansion of slavery.

The South believed that the North was using slavery as a tool to resurrect the Federalist Party and further the central government at the expense of states' rights. This was the catalyst that propelled 11 states to attempt secession from the Union. This precipitated the Civil War.

With the election of Abraham Lincoln, who ran on a message of containing slavery to where it currently existed, and the success of the Republican Party to which he belonged – the first entirely regional party in US history – in that election, South Carolina seceded on December 20, 1860, the first state to ever officially secede from the United States. Four months later, Georgia, Florida, Alabama, Mississippi, Texas and

Louisiana seceded as well. Later Virginia (except for its Northwestern counties, which broke away and formed the Union-loyal state of West Virginia), Arkansas, North Carolina, and Tennessee joined them. The people of the seceded states elected Jefferson Davis as president of the newly formed Southern Confederacy.

The potato famine that struck Ireland and Germany in the 1840s–1850s sent waves of hungry immigrants to America's shores. More of them settled in the North than in the South, where the existence of slavery depressed wages. These newcomers had sought refuge in the *United* States, not in New York or Virginia or Louisiana. To most of them, the U.S. was a single entity, not a collection of sovereign nations, and arguments in favor of secession failed to move them, for the most part.

From Articles of Confederation to "A More Perfect Union." Many people, especially those wishing to support the South's right to secede in 1860–61, have said that when 13 American colonies rebelled against Great Britain in 1776, it was an act of secession. Others say the two situations were different and the colonies' revolt was a revolution. The war resulting from that colonial revolt is known as the American Revolution or the American War for Independence. During that war, each of the rebelling colonies regarded itself as a sovereign nation, cooperating with a dozen other sovereigns in a relationship of convenience to achieve shared goals, the most immediate being independence from Britain. On Nov.

15, 1777, the Continental Congress passed the Articles of Confederation — "Certain Articles of Confederation and Perpetual Union"— to create "The United States of America." That document asserted that "Each State retains is sovereignty, freedom and independence" while entering into "a firm league of friendship with each other" for their common defense and to secure their liberties, as well as to provide for "their mutual and general welfare."

The Emancipation Proclamation was one of the most brilliant political moves in history in my estimation. In addition to freeing all the slaves in areas of rebellion, it also prevented Union military officers from returning runaway slaves to their masters, as well as stopping intervention from Europe on the behalf of the slave states. It is important to note that this action didn't actually free the slaves, and that not until the passing of the 13th Amendment were these slaves legally free.

John Brown – Freedom Vigilante

John Brown from Torrington, Connecticut, by way of Ohio, was instilled with a strong belief in the Bible and a strong hatred of slavery. Often seeking the company of blacks, he even lived in a freedman's community in North Elba, New York, for two years. He became a conductor in the Underground Railroad and organized a self-protection league for freemen of color and fugitive slaves.

As with today, there are always the oppressed, having what can only be referred to as 'Stockholm Syndrome'

– siding with and/or defending their oppressors. John Brown's first raid, Sunday, October 16, 1859, would reveal such an individual in 'Hayward Shepherd' – a black baggage handler who was the first casualty of this campaign. He was killed trying to defend the 'Baltimore & Ohio' railroad station from Brown's secret attack.

The Raid On Harpers Ferry

Nearly 1,000 miles northeast of Mobile, on the night of October 16, 1859, John Brown—the radical abolitionist who had killed proslavery settlers in Kansas—led 21 men in a raid to capture the U.S. arsenal at Harpers Ferry, Virginia (now West Virginia).

After seizing Hall's Rifle Works, as well as the arsenal and armory, Brown captured about 60 prominent men of the area to hold as hostages,, one of whom happened to be a great-grandnephew of George Washington, Lewis Washington. He also attempted to enlist the slaves of these hostages – the intent to set them free (possibly to create a militia), but to his dismay, none would join him.

Initial reaction in the South was that this was the work of a small group of fanatics, but when Northern newspapers, authors and legislators began praising him as a martyr—a poem by John Greenleaf Whittier eulogizing Brown was published in the New York Herald Tribune less than a month after the execution— their actions were taken as further proof that Northern abolitionists wished to carry out genocide of white

Southerners. These flames were fanned higher as information came out that Brown had talked to other abolitionists, including Frederick Douglass, about his plans and even received financial assistance from some of them.

Brown Sentenced To Death

Though Brown denied it, his plan was to use the arsenal's weapons to arm a slave uprising. He and his followers, 16 white men and five black ones, holed up in the arsenal after they were discovered, and were captured there by a group of U.S. Marines commanded by an Army lieutenant colonel, Robert E. Lee.

Brown had denied any plan "to excite or incite the slaves to rebellion or to make insurrection." He never intended to commit murder or treason or to destroy property, he claimed—though earlier that year he had purchased several hundred pikes and some firearms. By the time he was 50 years old, Brown was convinced God had selected him as the champion to lead slaves into freedom, and if that required the use of force, well, that was God's will, too.

"Now if it is deemed necessary that I should forfeit my life for the furtherance of the ends of justice, and mingle my blood further with the blood of my children and with the blood of millions in this slave country whose rights are disregarded by wicked, cruel, and unjust enactments, I say let it be done," he said.

These "unjust enactments" included the Constitution,

the Missouri Compromise of 1820, the Kansas-Nebraska Act, and the Supreme Court's ruling in the Dred Scott decision of 1857.

He was tried and convicted for murder, conspiracy to incite a slave uprising, and treason against the Commonwealth of Virginia. He was hanged at Charles Town, the county seat near Harpers Ferry, on December 2. Among those watching the execution, "with unlimited, undeniable contempt" for Brown, was the future assassin of President Abraham Lincoln, John Wilkes Booth.

This failed attempt was pivotal in the abolitionist movement as it was one of the first times a white man put his life, and the life of his family and friends on the line for blacks. Many talked the talk, but he walked the walk.

The Beginnings of the Underground Railroad

The origin of the 'Underground Railroad' can be traced back to before the American Revolution. Even before the 1800s, a system to abet runaways seems to have existed. George Washington complained in 1786 that one of his runaway slaves was aided by "a society of Quakers, formed for such purposes." Quakers, more correctly called the Religious Society of Friends, were among the earliest abolition groups. Their influence may have been part of the reason Pennsylvania, where many Quakers lived, was the first state to ban slavery.

Two Quakers, Levi Coffin and his wife Catherine, are believed to have aided over 3,000 slaves to escape over a period of years. For this reason, Levi is sometimes called the president of the Underground

Railroad.

Any involvement with this Underground Railroad or freeing of slaves resulted in extreme punishments as previously stated, in the forms of whippings, burnings, hangings or jail-time. These punishments were also meted out as fines ranging from hundreds to thousands of dollars in addition to the stiff jail time. In contrast, states with strong abolitionist support operated their veins of the underground system openly and freely. Stephen Myers, founder of 'Northern Star and Freemen's Advocate', became one of the most important figures in this underground movement adding to the formation of 'Vigilance Committees' who's purpose was to help slaves escape captivity.

This action was offset by vigilante groups who periodically took the law in their own hands, administering wild-west justice to whomever they pleased.

Once free, Always Free - Dred Scott

Before there was Dred Scott, in 1824, there was Winny vs. Whiteside, the result of who's decision established the "once free, always free" standard. This was in fact, the basis upon which Dred Scott placed his hope. It was the division of the states over slavery that created the dichotomy of free and slave states under the same constitution.

Dred Scott was born around 1800. A slave for most of his life, he was instrumental in the establishment of free slaves in America. His then master, Peter Blow, moved to St. Louis, Missouri in 1830, taking his slaves with him.

The United States Ordinance of 1787 prohibited slavery in the Northwest Territory, but Illinois' state constitution included the phrase, "Neither slavery nor involuntary servitude shall herein by introduced into this state otherwise than for the punishment of crimes." This wording allowed for the retaining of slaves, circumventing the prohibition of slavery in the state well into the 19th century.

After Scott got married to Harriett Robinson, his then owner Dr. Emerson moved him and his new wife to Louisiana, after his own marriage to Eliza Irene Sanford.

Filing Suit For His Freedom

Upon the death of Emerson in 1843, Scott, hired out by Emerson's widow, tries to arrange freedom for himself and his wife offering $300. When the widow refused, Scott took the matter to court citing that they both had lived in a free territory for an extended period of time and, that he lived in a free state. The 'once free, always free' established by the aforementioned Winny v. Whitesides decision meant that because the couple had lived for extended periods in a free territory, and he had lived in a free state, their petitions claimed they were free. This, the first trial, in June 1847, was tossed out because he couldn't prove he and his wife were owned by Mrs. Emerson. The retrial, in 1850 granted the couple their freedom for two years, after which time it was rescinded.

The pro-slavery Missouri state Supreme Court's

justices sought ways to overturn the advances made on behalf of free slaves in the region. This is also one of the first instances that legally raised the question of state's rights as opposed to the authority of the U.S. Congress to prohibit slavery in the territories.

When Scott's appeal to the United States Circuit Court in Missouri was denied, Scott and his lawyers then appealed to the Supreme Court.

Of the nine justices, five were from slave-holding families and in the spirit of the old south, Mrs. Emerson's brother, John Sanford of New York, claimed he now owned the slaves even though he and the plaintiff were from different states. This most important discrepancy shifted the focus of the case to actual jurisdiction - the Supreme Court, or was Scott a citizen of the United States?

This argument would serve to strengthen Abraham Lincoln's political platform as in 1857, the majority opinion stated that because of Scott's race he was not a citizen and had no right to sue under the Constitution.

Dred Scott Finally Gets His Freedom

One of the biggest mysteries of this pivotal case is the fact that much of Dred's legal fees were paid by the sons of his original owner, Peter Blow. After failing to obtain his freedom through the courts, they purchased Dred and Harriet Scott for,$750 and then 0set them free.

Harriet Beecher Stowe: Abolitionist and Author

Another one of the many pivotal occurrences catapulting the Civil War was Harriet Beecher Stowe's 'Uncle Tom's Cabin' which shed a negative light on Southern slavery. Stowe, an abolitionist who had come to know a number of escaped slaves while she was living in Cincinnati, authored the novel that presented a scathing view of this Southern slavery system,
In 1852, her melodramatic depictions of slave life put on display the horrors of the Southern slavery system through scenes such as those of Eliza, who escaped captivity by way of an icy Ohio River. Many believe her stories to be from first-hand accounts of the slaves she interviewed in Cincinnati. For example:

"The huge green fragment of ice on which she alighted pitched and creaked as her weight came on it but she stayed there not a moment. With wild cries and desperate energy she leaped to another and still another cake; stumbling, leaping, slipping, springing upwards again! Her shoes are gone her stockings cut from her feet while blood marked every step; but she saw nothing, felt nothing, till dimly, as in a dream, she saw the Ohio side and a man helping her up the bank."

Harriet Beecher Stowe is by proxy, the product of her father, Rev. Dr. Lyman Beecher's involvement in the Christian revival movement's Second Awakening which inspired social activism. He also preached against slavery in response to the Missouri Compromise.

In 1836, Harriet married widowed clergyman Calvin Ellis Stowe, a professor at her father's theological seminary. They had seven children between 1836 and 1850. During their time in Cincinnati, the Stowes met and talked with slaves that had escaped to Ohio from neighboring Kentucky and Virginia. They were friends with abolitionists who participated in the Underground Railroad, and Harriet visited Kentucky, where she saw the impact of slavery first-hand.

"I wrote what I did because as a woman, as a mother, I was oppressed and broken-hearted with the sorrows and injustice I saw, because as a Christian I felt the dishonor to Christianity – because as a lover of my country, I trembled at the coming day of wrath."

In 1839, the Stowes hired a servant girl from Kentucky, who by the laws of Ohio was free since her mistress had brought her and allowed her to stay in Cincinnati. However, a few months later, they learned that the girl's master was in town looking for her and could legally, by any means, seize her and return her to slavery in Kentucky. One night, Professor Stowe and his brother-in-law, Henry Ward Beecher, armed themselves and drove the girl in a covered wagon by unfrequented roads into the country to a trusted friend's home. This incident became the basis of the fugitives' escape in Uncle Tom's Cabin.

In 1851 Stowe began a contract with The National Era, an anti-slavery magazine, for a story that would "paint a word picture of slavery," for Northerners who had never witnessed it first-hand, as a way to galvanize them to action against the institution of slavery. Stowe originally planned for the story to consist of just three or four installments, but she ended up writing more than 40. The first installment was published June 5, 1851, and before the series was finished, she had an offer to publish it as a novel.

Stowe continued her various philanthropic efforts to help slaves, including establishing schools for them, and continued to write articles and columns for newspapers, and novels. When the American Civil War began, Harriet felt that President Abraham Lincoln did not move quickly enough to emancipate slaves and met with him in 1862 to urge him to take decisive action.

The novel has a more infamous reputation of having popularized many stereotypes that people still carry today. Some have even said that the book is seen more often in a negative light because of creating so many stereotypes that some people underestimate and even forget the novel's powerful role as an anti-slavery tool. In any event, Uncle Tom's Cabin would become the image of the black man whose influence still lingers today.

Critics pointed out that Stowe had never been to the South, but her novel became a bestseller in the North (banned in the South) and the most effective bit of propaganda to come out of the abolitionist movement. It galvanized many who had been sitting on the sidelines. Reportedly, when President Abraham Lincoln met Stowe during the Civil War he said to her, "So you're the little woman who started this big war." Frederick Douglas

The most famous black abolitionist was Frederick Douglass, formerly Frederick Bailey. An intellectual, he wrote many papers, and worked for newspapers and other publications as well. One such publication was William Lloyd Garrison's newspaper, 'The Liberator'. After returning from a trip to Great Britain, he founded the black abolitionist paper, The North Star whose title referenced the escaped slaves route to freedom in the Northern states and Canada - just follow the North Star.

Douglass toured as an example and storyteller telling audiences of his experiences as a slave. The freedom and equality he experienced in England was something he had never experienced and he wanted that kind of freedom to exist for Blacks in the states.
Martin R. Delaney, who worked with Douglas on the North Star was one of three black men accepted into Harvard Medical School. These three were subsequently petitioned out of their positions by the students, who didn't want to attend school with Blacks. The success of Uncle Tom's Cabin prompted Delaney to write and publish his own experiences.

Harriet Tubman and The Underground Railroad

While Sojourner Truth, Douglass, Delaney and others wrote and spoke to end slavery, a former slave named Harriet Tubman, (Harriet Ross), was actively leading slaves to freedom. After escaping from bondage herself, she made repeated trips into Dixie to help others. Believed to have helped some 300 slaves to escape, she was noted for warning those she was assisting that she would shoot any of them who turned back, because they would endanger herself and others she was assisting.

Tubman was an agent of the Underground Railroad, a system of "safe houses" and way stations that secretly helped runaways. The trip might begin by hiding in the home, barn or other location owned by a Southerner opposed to slavery, and continuing from place to place until reaching safe haven in a free state or Canada. Those who reached Canada did not have to fear being returned under the Fugitive Slave Act. Several communities and individuals claim to have created the term "Underground Railroad." In the southern section of states on the north bank of the Ohio River, a "reverse underground railroad" operated; blacks in those states were kidnapped, whether they had ever been slaves or not, and taken South to sell through a series of clandestine locations.

Tubman is also lauded as the first American woman to have led a military raid on American soil. She orchestrated one of the most important and daring covert operations in US history. In South Carolina, 1863, Tubman heard about a mission by General David Hunter of the Union Army to recruit slaves to help them fight the Confederacy. The problem was that the Combahee River was fortified with mines, creating an untraversable barrier. If the general couldn't disable the mines, he couldn't free the slaves he needed to fortify his military stance. Tubman knows that the mines were planted by slaves under orders from Conference military officials and if she can find the slaves who planted them, the mines could be disabled. Harriet Tubman, under cover of nightfall, went behind enemy lines, tracked down the slaves who planted the mines and learned their locations. She then brought the information back General Hunter. He then sent Tubman, and Union soldiers on a raid to liberate slaves by disabling the mines, setting fire to the fields and during the chaos, freeing and rounding up the fleeing slaves. Hunter and Tubman applied the information to successfully free over 700 former slaves to recruit into the Union army.

Slaves might have been one of the main reasons for the Civil War but they were also at least one of the reasons the Union won.

CHAPTER 7

HIDDEN COLORS

The compromise was that she retained at least some of the chains, which they allowed to be kept around her feet.

7 HIDDEN COLORS

Frederick August Bartholdi & the Statue of Liberty

The icon of America's freedom, the Statue of Liberty is significant for at least two reasons: She marked the end of slavery in the US and she served as a beacon of hope for all who saw her. This is evidenced by the inscription on her front panel:

"Give me your tired, your poor, your huddled masses yearning to breathe free, The wretched refuse of your teeming shore. Send these, the homeless, tempest-tossed to me, I lift my lamp beside the golden door!"

This poem by Emma Lazarus, begins by comparing Lady liberty to the Colosus of Rhodes. I believe that her words point to the need for America to balance out the population and workforce, which was being somewhat overrun by the ex-slaves entering society and into the paid workplace. I'm not insinuating that this was the purpose of the poem, it just seems that this section was chosen as an invitation of needed fodder to aid in the maintenance of the previous status quo. It just seems like a desperate call toward the influx of those of European descent to stem the tide of former slave domination.

Our chosen beacon of hope had another beginning. In

honor of the completion of the Suez Canal, Frederick August Bartholdi, along with others submitted designs for a statuesque lighthouse that would grace its entrance at Fort Said. The drawings he submitted were of a veiled Egyptian woman fashioned after the previously mentioned statue of Colosus of Rhodes which stood on the Greek island of Rhodes. To his dismay, they rejected his design, opting for a more conservative lighthouse.

It was previously accepted that the original rendition of the Statue of Liberty was the image of an African looking woman that was, for whatever reason, rejected by the committee responsible for her placement. My thoughts on this is that the original presentation would have caused a greater divide of the recently torn United States, and that the South would have considered it an insult (much like how blacks feel about the Confederate flag).

When Bartholdi was approached by France to create a statue representing the freeing of the slaves, he immediately offered them a variation of the statue he'd offered Egypt. The commission is said to have come from French abolitionists in celebration of the slaves having been freed so he presented a modified version of the Egyptian (black-ish) woman Egypt had rejected. The statue was clearly a woman who possessed Afroid features in a flowing white gown holding chains in her left hand. America refused the first statue, saying that they didn't want a black woman representing America for all eternity. They opted for his re-design, an European looking woman with a book in her left hand and a torch in her right hand raised above her head ala the Colosus. The compromise was that she retained at least some of the chains, which they allowed to be kept around her feet.

The report of the National Parks Service says that this is just another urban myth, even though they concede that the original concept was the depiction of a Black-ish woman. This just seems like the age-old misdirection. It is again, having to take the word of chosen 'experts' and their interpretations of these facts. Do I actually have to be told what I'm seeing with my own eyes? It is, as I previously wrote, a fact that George Zimmerman was clearly the aggressor in the Trevon Martin case, substantiated by the audio evidence at the scene. Am I supposed to accept the experts' finding of Zimmerman innocent of murder charges - even though I see with my own eyes that a murder, or at least manslaughter, did occur?

However, I, like you, have to come to my own conclusions based on facts and conjecture. Our Statue of Liberty does, in fact, represent different things to different people.

World War II

In order to fully understand the Second World War, one has to understand the origin of the Jewish race. As previously stated, the original Jews were brown, or olive-complexioned. Aside from their traditions and practices, this was a defining factor in how they were seen, received and treated.

The Jewish rise to power stemmed from nepotism and exclusion. The Jews also understood that the prices of goods and services were founded on principles of free enterprise – that products should always be sold for what the market would bare, and not what they were worth – free from government intervention. This was in fact different from the barter system adapted from the Silk Road. The Jews had become financial titans in Europe and had established an advantage in commerce.

This advantage was seen as unfair by the German population as these Jews began to ascend socially and politically. The rise of the Jew angered many German citizens as they saw it as the Jews erasing their culture and stealing their heritage and birthright. The older Germans, the common folk with whom I've spoken, speak of the rhetoric and propaganda against inferior races and cultures taking over a proud German nation.

This propaganda appeared also in the forms of articles and visual support/examples like depicting a Black woman hugging an 'Aryan' girl with the caption "The result! A loss of racial pride." (US Holocaust Memorial Museum).

The Jew may have been the headline, but Melanin became the story. Let me explain: When someone wants to create a race of blond-haired, blue-eyed beings, they must remove (or minimize) melanin from the equation. The color of brown and Black people comes from melanin, so if one wants to remove color from being introduced into future generations, one must eliminate the source or sources of this perceived anomaly. Since we know that the original Jews were brown as well, it can be deduced that nepotism was not the only factor in the decision to eliminate them. It seems that it is just not newsworthy to mention the many Blacks who were also killed in the name of ethnic cleansing during the Second World War.

Interestingly, prior to 1890, interracial marriage was allowed in Germany. The subsequent eugenics controversy sparked opposition as this mingling was said to have had detrimental effects on the quality of the German race because mixed-race children were seen as inferior stock. Again, politics and economics came into focus as the mixed-race children would be German citizens and would therefore possess the rights of White Germans to vote, serve in the military, occupy government positions and hold public office.

Post World War I sentiment toward mixed marriage in the German colonies of Africa was separatism. Even Ghandi spoke out against interracial mingling saying that the 'Kafir' (another word for nigger) was inferior and lazy. (He did not want his countrymen to be grouped with these 'inferior' Africans) The Reichstag (German Parliament) promoted apartheid and forbade the intertwining of races in the German-occupied colonies by law which they also applied to the German citizens and Allied soldiers in Rheinland during that time. So, after the First World War and the Treaty of Versailles, the Allies liberated Germany's African colonies and sent those Germans who were there, (die Schutztruppen) back to Germany. These returning Germans brought with them the racist, separatist views of those German-occupied African colonies. This prompted the German Reichstag to enact laws forbidding the mixing of the black and white races stating eugenics or racial purity as the foundation. They labeled the Black soldiers as rapists and thugs (much like today) and subsequently, inferior to the German race. The propaganda also said they were carriers of venereal and other diseases and were responsible for the "Rheinland Bastards", the progeny of Black soldiers and German women. The propaganda of the small, seemingly insignificant new Nazi movement was that racial mixing was a threat to the purity of the Germanic race. Even In *Mein Kampf* (My Struggle), Hitler wrote that "*the Jews had brought the Negroes into the Rhineland with the clear aim of ruining the hated white race by the necessarily-resulting bastardization.*"

African-German children or 'Afro-Germans' as they are widely known, were usually marginalized in German society and faced social and economic sanctions. For example, they weren't even allowed to attend university and were prohibited from seeking most jobs, receiving medical treatment or serving in the military.

The Blacks and Afro-Germans became a target of the rising Nazi Party and were targeted with racial and population policies. The Gestapo (German Secret State Police), by 1937, had secretly rounded up and forcibly sterilized many of them, subjected others to medical experiments, and others somehow, just mysteriously disappeared.

Actually, some of the medical experiments coincide with the Olympic Games of 1936 wherein 18 Black athletes were allowed to compete (not by the host country Germany, but the International Olympic Committee) and annihilated the Olympic records, as well as the competition. The physical prowess of these seemingly super-human athletes sparked curiosity about their genetic makeup, as it disagreed with the perceived genetic inferiority suggested by eugenicists.

Germans of African descent were also victims. Coming from all economic and social backgrounds, after World War II, they were the targets of systemic racism, which included torture and murder.

A great many Black people in Nazi Germany from 1933 to 1945 also had to endure the same persecution, medical experimentation, brutality, isolation, sterilization, incarceration and murder as the Jews. These victims included former soldiers, colonial officials, students, artists and entertainers. Many of whom were killed or detained in internment camps of note included: Dancer Lari Gilges (married to a German woman) murdered by the SS; American female Jazz artist Valaida Snow (imprisoned in Axis); The artist Josef Nassy (detained in the Beverloo transit camp in Belgium as an enemy alien) who was later transferred to Laufen. Other notables whom we know endured the concentration camps included: Lionel Romney, a sailor in the US Merchant Marine; Jean Marcel Nicolas, a Haitian national; Jean Voste, an African Belgian; and Bayume Mohamed Hussein from Tanganyika (or Tanzania as it's known today) who died in the Sachsenhausen camp, near Berlin. Many more Blacks were incarcerated in Gestapo prisons and concentration camps. A lot of these Black soldiers of the French, American and British were worked to death on construction projects, mistreated in these

Nazi POW or concentration camps, or, immediately killed by the SS or Gestapo. Even though the evidence points to the contrary, it is still reported that there was not a systematic program for the elimination of Blacks in Germany during this time.

Though history doesn't recognize the mass extermination of Black people by Nazi Germany, it is clear that they also suffered greatly in mass quantities under this racist regime. Black people were at the bottom of the racial scale of non-Aryans along with Jews and Romani/Roma people and therefore, experienced discrimination in employment, welfare, and housing. Barred from pursuing a higher education, they were socially isolated and forbidden to have sexual relations and marriages with Aryans by law.

So, the propaganda of the "Black Horror on the Rhine"' told of the uncivilized Black African soldiers raping and impregnating innocent German women the result of which were these so-called "Rhineland Bastards". The actual, local opinions of the soldiers were that they were "courteous and often popular...". Still, these 400-600 ill-born children were used as fodder to fuel anti-race-mixing sentiment. This anti-Black view was further supported by the tie-in from Hitler's "Mein Kampf" which said these children were contaminating the white race. He also said (slightly different from above) "*Jews were responsible for bringing Negroes into the Rhineland, with the ultimate idea of bastardizing the white race which they hate and thus lowering its cultural and political level so that the Jew might dominate."*

(This viewpoint was also echoed by Henry Ford and Thomas Edison in regard to the influence of Black inspired music.) He continued by implying that this was a plot on the part of the French, because the French population was becoming *"negrified"*. As a direct result of these children (German citizens by right), a special Gestapo commission was created and charged with "the discrete sterilization of the Rhineland bastards", with Hitler's approval. Approximately 500 children were sterilized under this program, including girls as young as 11. Also, during this time, there were reportedly between 20,000 to 30,000 Blacks residing in Germany, so that the estimation of the 400-600 children seems a little low. However, beyond the forced sterilization program in the Rhineland, there seemed to have been no reported open Nazi policy towards Afro-Germans.

Although no orders were issued in regard to black prisoners of war, many German commanders separated black soldiers from captured French units for summary execution. It is important to note however that as there was no official policy, the treatment of black prisoners of war varied widely, and most captured black soldiers were taken prisoner rather than executed. However, in many prisoner of war camps, black soldiers were kept segregated from white, and generally experienced far worse treatment than their white cellmates.

I'm saying all this to make it clear that one of the primary focuses of the Nazi Regime was to eliminate Black people and those people with Black in them from the German equation – thus, the blonde hair and blue eyes. The characteristics of those they found to be inferior or impure 'lower races' were those of Black people including facial features, hair type and perceived intelligence quotients. Remember, Blacks joined the Jews in those concentration and extermination camps. So, even though they weren't Jews, Slavs or Romani, under a supplementary decree, they were still considered an inferior race and subject to the Nuremberg Laws.

Slavery Sentiment in the 20th Century

As before mentioned, after the War of 1812, the slaveholding states were afraid of insufficient Congressional representation which would weaken their property and trade positions. The Missouri Compromise of 1820 sought through the U.S. Senate and House of Representatives to regulate the balance of power between free and slaveholding states.

State's Rights remained an issue well into the 20th century when in 1948, a group of Southern delegates walked out of the Democratic National Convention. This resulted in the formation of the 'State's Rights

Party', or 'Dixiecrats'. The reason for the split in the normally conservative Democratic Party was the call for more liberal federal anti-lynching legislation. Add to that the fight against racial discrimination by establishing a permanent Fair Employment Practices Committee, eliminating poll taxes, and the desegregation of the military. These practices were part of the fabric of racial discrimination that made the Civil Rights Bill necessary. It was the liberal democrats' lobbying for anti-lynching legislation, desegregation of America's military, the establishment of the Fair Employment Practices Committee, and eliminating federal election poll taxes (which are known to have been established to deter African Americans from the voting process).

In 1948, Strom Thurmond and the States Rights Party opposed federally mandated desegregation and anti-discrimination laws. Four years later, 'Brown vs. Board of Education' found these 'separate but equal' practices to be unconstitutional, sparking States Rights demonstrations. In other words, State's Rights was a rallying cry for keeping the machine of racism alive. The old-boy network believed that inequality, and the murder and subjugation of blacks were not just ok, they were necessary for a better America - natural selection as it were.

CHAPTER 8

UNIONS

After the Civil war, the freed slaves began to enter into the paid labor force and literally took it by storm.

8 UNIONS

Pre-Civil War

Let's dial it back to pre- Civil War America when 80% of free white men were shop-keepers, land owners, farmers and craftsmen who owned, or held the land they worked. This society of property holders and independent producers suffered a tremendous loss of status as a result of the Civil War.

What we need to understand is that pre-Civil war, land was capital – it was money. U. S. currency was based on land holdings, just like today. The more land one held, the more political power he or she wielded and, the more collateral for goods and services, access and privilege.

Post-Civil War

History seems to have forgotten that after the Civil War it wasn't just poor Southern whites and immigrants who saturated the workplace, it was also freed slaves. Since freed slaves worked for reduced wages, the immigrants and poor whites also had to accept reduced wages (not as low as the ex-slaves, but reduced nonetheless), what they referred to as 'slave wages' (because, that's what the former slaves would accept). In fact, that's where we get that term.

After the Civil war, the freed slaves began to enter into the paid labor force and literally took it by storm. In fact, is not widely known that 40-50% of all Cowboys were Black. Working longer hours, for less pay, they became the new standard of labor and changed the employment landscape. Add to that the influx of immigrants from southern and eastern Europe and the labor market suddenly becomes over-saturated with unskilled workers, who replaced the skilled craftsmen. The result of this phenomenon is a significant wage decrease and a halted growth of working-class income. Manufacturing was in full swing and the expanding factories served to widen the chasm between owners or management, and employees.

The phrase " a fair day's wages for a fair day's work" came as a result of these immigrants and former slaves 'taking what they could get' working the longer hours for fewer wages. This also prompted the demand for an eight hour workday, as the former slaves and immigrants not only accepted, but we're used to a longer working day. This resulted in agitation for immigration restrictions both as employees and those entering the country. Most organizations restricted black membership through higher entry fees, outrageous technical exams, and unfair discriminatory practices such as the process of 'Grandfathering'.

For whatever reason, the history books have all but removed the former slave from this narrative, even though they comprised a significant portion of this new labor force.

Industrial Work

Most industrial workers put in 10 hr days/ 6 days per week at about $1.50 per day. For example, steelworkers worked 12 hr days, 7 days a week. HARSH. There were also an average of 35,000 dead (500,000 injured) per year in industrial accidents with no workers' compensation. By 1890, the richest 9 percent of Americans held nearly three-quarters of all wealth in the United States. But by 1900, one American in eight (nearly 10 million people) lived below the poverty line.

Three severe depressions -- 1873-1879, 1882-1885, and 1893-1897 (the worst of the three) -- rocked the economy in the last third of the century. With hard times came fierce competition as managers searched frantically for ways to cut costs. By 1900, two-thirds of all industrial work took place in large-scale mills such as Homestead. Industrial work featured the use of machines for mass production; the division of labor into intricately organized menial tasks; and the dictatorship of the clock.

The 10 hr a day, 6 days per week industrial worker rarely saw the owners of these facilities. The foreman or supervisor exercised complete authority over the unskilled workers in his section, hiring and firing them at will, even setting their wages. During the 1870s and 1880s, Frederick W. Taylor undertook time and motion studies of workers in steel mills with the aim of higher productivity and prices. He set up standard procedures and offered monetary incentives for beating production quotas. On one occasion, he designed 15 different ore shovels, each for a separate task. Soon, one hundred and forty men were doing the work of 600."Taylorism" was a philosophy adopted by many industries.

Many workers regarded themselves as citizens of a democratic republic. They expected to earn a "competence" -- enough money to support and educate their families and enough time to stay abreast of current affairs. Few but highly skilled workers could realize such democratic dreams. More and more, labor was managed as another part of an integrated system of industry however, ordinary workers refused to perform as cogs. In a variety of ways they sought to exert some control. Workers took off on traditional Holy Days (holidays), or Saints Days, or did not come into work on "Blue Monday". Or, they slowed down the grueling pace or simply walked off the job. Come spring, factories often reported turnover of 200 and 300 percent.

The American Dream

Most American workers believed in the American dream. As bad as their conditions were, they were better than the conditions in Europe, from where many had recently arrived. Workers also experienced a greater sense of opportunity (ie. free libraries, public schools, etc.) Many workers also experienced some improvement and social mobility. In one study, about one-fourth of manual laborers in Pittsburgh entered the lower middle class in their own life times. More often, such workers climbed or ascended in financial status within their own class. This is one explanation as to why American labor did not readily embrace radical visions such as socialism. Most workers, seeing some improvement, believed in the American dream of success, even if they did not fully share it.

It took $600 per year to make ends meet in the late 1800's and most industrial workers made approximately $500 annually. Women and children therefore had to go to work. By 1900, 1.7 million children were working and on average, children worked 60 hours per week and took home pay that was a third the size of adult males. Only 5% of married women held jobs outside the home in 1900. Many women involved in the garment industry worked in their homes, cutting and sewing garments (sweat shops) Married black women were four times more likely to work outside of the home (as domestics, etc.) than their white counterparts. Industrialization pushed women into industries considered an extension of housework: food processing, textiles, clothing, cigar making, and domestic service.

Working class Americans did improve their overall lot. Though the gap between rich and poor widened, between 1860 and 1890, real daily wages climbed 50%, more the result of declining prices than of increases in pay. The number of hours worked declined after 1890. Yet most unskilled and semi-skilled workers in factories continued to receive the low pay of $500 per year. (A skilled worker made about twice the pay of an unskilled worker). But, while some of these workers enjoyed their advances, African American men faced discrimination. They were often used as strike-breakers, or were employed in service trades – waiting on whites in restaurants and trains.

This could even be referred to as the 'American Anti-Dream'. This is in fact, where 'tipping' began. These former slaves and other minorities, forced to take these service jobs did so without receiving payment. The owners of these establishments didn't want to pay these workers so the elite were encouraged to tip them. It is however important to note that Whites who were forced to take these positions received higher tips than minorities, which, in many places, is still true today.

Early Unions:

Even before the Civil War Unions began forming. Skilled craft workers – carpenters, iron molders and cigar makers – who joined together to protect themselves. Railroad brotherhoods also furnished insurance for those hurt or killed on RR lines. Largely local, predominantly white and exclusively male, these early craft unions remained weak and unconnected to each other, as well as to other unskilled workers. The construct of a few of these new unions shared these attributes, but were dissimilar in many other ways. One underlying thrust was their desire to create natural, national alliances.

National Labor Union (NLU)

The National Labor Union (NLU), was initially formed by a group of craft unions, brotherhoods, and reformers. It reached out to both skilled and unskilled alike to create a nationwide organization. The NLU attacked the wage system as unfair and degrading, and, they urged workers to manage their own factories. As the NLU pushed energetically for an 8-hour day, ranks swelled to more than 600,000 but wilted during the depression that began in 1873 and the Great Railroad strike of 1877.

This Great Railroad strike of 1877, which began as a strike against the B + O Railroad, spread from Wheeling West Virginia to Pittsburgh and Chicago and turned violent. State militias were called out in states and fired on workers. Workers destroyed railroad property (most notably in Pittsburgh), so the President sent troops to break the strike. In the minds of many middle class people, unions and strikes became associated with violent, unruly radicalism.

Knights of Labor

The Knights of Labor proved more successful than the NLU. Terrence Powderly revived the organization, which had been founded in 1869. The Knights called for one big union to embrace all those who produced: including skilled and unskilled labor, men and women, native and immigrant, all religions and races. (unfortunately, these coalitions of inherent differences proved unstable.) The Knights saw workers as producers who had been denied by monopolies and special privilege and access, the enjoyment and end result of the wealth they created. The aim of the Knights was to make each man his own employer. The Knights envisioned a cooperative economy of mines, factories, and railroads, owned and operated by workers, who would pool their resources and profits. These Knights did not accept as permanent the wage system and the division of society into owners and workers. They wanted workers to also be owners.

The Knights established more than 140 cooperative workshops, sponsored political candidates in 200 cities and towns, and pushed for short-term reform. They advocated the 8 hr day, government regulation of trusts, and abolition of child labor and of liquor (a precursor to prohibition).

Theoretically, Powderly opposed strikes, but during the mid-1880's, local chapters of the Knights staged some successful strikes against railroads. The Knights name however, was unfairly linked in the public mind to anarchists in the Haymarket Bombing incident of 1886 in Chicago and they thus lost a lot of support from middle class people. An unsuccessful strike against the Texas and Pacific Railroad further weakened the Knights and by the 1890s, the Knights teetered on the edge of extinction.

The American Federation of Labor

The Knights' position as the premier union in the nation was taken by the rival American Federation of Labor, or AF of L - a federation of independent craft unions led by Samuel Gompers, a former cigar maker. Whereas the Knights aimed to reform society, the AF of L focused on basic bread and butter issues for skilled workers. When Gompers was asked by a congressional committee to identify his goals for labor, he responded with one word: "*more.*"

Gompers accepted the division of society into owners and laborers. He accepted capitalism and the wage system, but sought better wages and working conditions, as well as shorter hours for skilled workers. The AF of L did not run candidates for office like the Knights, but rather supported candidates whom it judged friendly to labor. By 1901, it had more than a million members, almost a third of all skilled workers in the United States. Importantly, only two locals – the Cigar Makers' Union and the Typographers' Union -- enrolled women. As we mentioned before, most unions restricted black membership through high fees, technical exams, and discriminatory practices.

The American Railway Union (ARU)

The ARU was an Industrial Union led by Eugene Debs. It sought to organize all of the workers -- skilled and unskilled -- in the railroad industry. It was crushed during the Pullman Strike.

Just to let you know why unions and unionization were frowned upon by capitalists and government, here is the Constitution of the IWW (International Workers of the World):

The IWW Constitution:

"The working class and the employing class have nothing in common. There can be no peace so long as hunger and want are found among millions of the working people and the few, who make up the employing class, have all the good things of life.
Between these two classes a struggle must go on until the workers of the world organize as a class, take possession of the means of production, abolish the wage system, and live in harmony with the Earth.

Instead of the conservative motto, "A fair day's wage for a fair day's work," we must inscribe on our banner the revolutionary watchword, "Abolition of the wage system."

It is the historic mission of the working class to do away with capitalism. The army of production must be organized, not only for everyday struggle with capitalists, but also to carry on production when capitalism shall have been overthrown. By organizing industrially we are forming the structure of the new society within the shell of the old."

Is it just me or does this sound a little too much like communism? Is this one of the reasons unions were frowned upon?

Management Strikes Back

By 1900, only 10% of all industrial workers were members of a union. For many of these workers, unions were their systematic response to industrialization. Employers enjoyed advantages in labor confrontations, as they used "yellow dog" contracts, blacklists, lockouts, company spies, and strike-breakers dividing the workers by language, race, and gender. Raised to self-reliance, many working men and women resisted unionization. Individual workers coped by putting in more hours to save a few pennies, walked out in exhaustion or disgust, or, slowed down on the job. Take for example the Laundresses Strike in Richmond, Va., -- 3000 laundresses struck in 1881. Most of whom were black women from the Washing society. The strike was not successful.

Music Unions

As with many other unions, Music Unions were established to keep blacks, many of whom were superior players, out of higher paying jobs. That relegated these top musicians to the 'Chittlin' Circuit', such as 'The Macon', 'The Canabar' and 'My Brother's Place' (all in Columbus, Ohio). That was one of the main reasons Miles Davis disliked many whites – he was the best trumpeter on the planet and was not allowed to walk in the front doors of the places where his name was on the marquee and people packed the houses to see him. And, to top it off, jobs for which he was qualified were given to less-talented non-black players.

This was never more evident than in the world famous Cotton Club located in Harlem. To put it into perspective, imagine having a shed in your own backyard and being denied entry into this facility - even though it's right in the middle of your property. The reality of it is, that no one was allowed to enter the club or even work there unless he or she passed the *paper bag test*. They would actually hold up a brown paper bag to the face of the prospect and if the skin was darker than the bag, they weren't allowed entry. That is also why most of the blackish musicians who worked there also used Madam C. J. Walker's hair straightening iron or processing cream to straighten their hair. Whether the reason was that these individuals created a better mosaic or because of the perceived kindred because of the white blood coursing through their veins, the main point is that they were more accepted than darker skinned folks. Catch phrases like "if you're light bright or damn near white, then you're alright", "any shade of yellow is mellow" and "if you're black, get way back", really told the story. Many of those who were mixed also forbade their children from mingling and bearing children with those of a darker hue. So for many, bleaching cream was also the order of the day.

Conclusion

As different as their thrusts and focuses, these unions did share many similar ideals. Fair wages for a fair day's work, more representation in the workflow process, better benefits and profit-sharing and, limiting or preventing participation of minorities and former slaves.

CHAPTER 9

NATURAL SELECTION

Eugenics is the process, and practice of creating 'well-born', or genetically superior beings.

9 NATURAL SELECTION

Natural Selection

To understand the meaning behind Darwin's theory of 'Natural Selection', one needs to understand the hierarchy of the wild where the strong 'normally' overcome the weak. I put normally in quotes because it is not always true that the strong dominate the weak. There are so many other factors that come into play including of course, strength, cunning, ingenuity, ferocity, weaponry, experience, fear, tenacity, bravery, cowardice, size, possibility, resources, imagination, knowledge and creativity. It was Albert Einstein who said that imagination is more important than knowledge.

This was never more clear than the 'weak' slaves overcoming the 'strong' bonds of slavery. But indeed, t he strength it takes to exist as a slave is paled by the strength it takes to escape slavery. Their strength lies in the acquisition of 'Black Power' or, in other words, the processing of energy through carbon or melanin coupled with the burning desire to live freely.

So, these supposed inferior beings had the intestinal fortitude to overcome seemingly insurmountable, overwhelming odds. They used brains and brawn to usurp a foe that held strategic advantage and superior firepower. So, even though they were perceived as the weaker of the species, their human will and desire to breathe free spurred them forward.

Eugenics

Eugenics (/juːˈdʒɛnɪks/; from Greek εὐγενής eugenes "well-born" from εὖ eu, "good, well" and γένος genos, "race, stock, kin")[is a set of beliefs and practices that aims at improving the genetic quality of a group of individuals. Eugenics is the process, and practice of creating 'well-born', or genetically superior beings.

Although eugenics as understood today dates from the late 19th century, efforts to select matings in order to secure offspring with desirable traits date from ancient times. Even Plato's Republic (c. 378 BCE) depicts a society where efforts were undertaken to improve human beings through selective breeding. This idea of 'positive' eugenics dates back to or before ancient Greece where, as before mentioned, Plato, in order to produce what he called a 'guardian class', suggested selective mating to produce better human beings.

These early eugenicists seemed mostly concerned with how perceived intelligence related to social class and race. When one understands the difference between 'knowledgeable' and 'intelligence', he or she can see the broken stick by which humanity is measured. Intelligence is the ability to adapt or create, while being knowledgeable, or learned, is storing and regurgitating facts.

Francis Galton

The term 'Eugenics' was coined by Francis Galton, (Darwin's half-cousin, who also popularized the concept of *nature v's nurture* in the late 1800's).

Galton felt that the high birth rate of the poor was a threat to civilization and that the "higher" races must supplant the "lower." His views gave validity to those who believed in racial and class superiority. He published his observations and conclusions in his book *'Inquiries into Human Faculty and its Development'*. Galton argued that human character was attributed to genes, not environment or education.

Galton had endowed a research fellowship in eugenics in 1904 and, in his will, provided funds for a chair of eugenics at University College, London. The fellowship and later the chair were occupied by Karl Pearson, a brilliant mathematician who helped to create the science of biometry, the statistical aspects of biology. Pearson was a controversial figure who believed, like Galton, that environment had little to do with the development of mental or emotional qualities.

Academic Discipline

Eugenics became an academic discipline at many colleges and universities and received funding from many sources. Organizations were formed to win public support and sway opinion towards responsible eugenic values in sex and parenthood, including the British Eugenics Education Society of 1907 and the American Eugenics Society of 1921. Both sought support from leading clergymen on moral grounds and modified their message to meet religious ideals. In 1909 the Anglican clergymen William Inge and James Peile both wrote for the British Eugenics Education Society. Inge was an invited speaker at the famed 1921

International Eugenics Conference, which was also endorsed fully by the Roman Catholic Archbishop of New York at the time, Patrick Joseph Hayes.

This ideology of 'genetic determinism' all but eliminated circumstance as a catalyst for behavior. The fact that this theory has been added to the curriculum in many Universities and funded by major organizations points to a major source of racism as well. To explain, potential department heads and leaders leave these courses with a preconception of who will succeed or fail and are therefore biased in their handling, appointing and promoting of employees.

The most disputed aspect of eugenics has been the definition of "improvement" of the human gene pool, such as what is a beneficial characteristic and what is a defect? This aspect of eugenics has historically been tainted with scientific racism. The real question is, what part does heredity play in the scheme of things? Heredity

The basic laws of what we call heredity were discovered, or uncovered by the man said to be the father of modern genetics Gregor Mendel (Mendelian inheritance) in 1865. He experimented with peas and found that each physical trait could be attributed to a combination of two units, called 'genes' which could be passed on from one generation to another. The results of these experiments formed the basis of eugenic theory, influencing scientists to attempt human improvement through selective breeding.

We can cite many articles and publications championing the idea and concept of selective breeding based on class, social status, and perceived intelligence, including: 'City of the Sun' by 'Tommaso Campanella' – 1623; and, 'Hereditary Genius' by Francis Galton – 1869; 'Development of a Eugenic Philosophy' a journal article by Frederick Osborn – 1937. This article, by Osborn called eugenics a social philosophy with major implications for social order. His ideas incorporated both positive and negative eugenics principles. He advocated for increased rates of sexual reproduction among those with desired qualities, and for those with less desirable traits, sterilization, or at least, reduced sexual reproduction.

Positive Eugenics v's 'Negative' Eugenics

Eugenic policies have been conceptually divided into two categories - 'Positive Eugenics' and 'Negative Eugenics'. Positive eugenics targets reproduction among the 'genetically advantaged'; for example, the mating of the intelligent, the healthy, and the successful. There are many methods to this end including financial and political rewards, targeted demographic analyses, in vitro fertilization, egg transplants, and cloning.

The perceived benefits of positive eugenics include increases in the population of the 'ruling class'. Positive eugenics is said to enhance the race of betters who, when mixed with other betters, increase the potential to properly govern or rule the 'lessers'.

Another way to promote positive eugenics is through access and privilege. People of means create sanctuaries for those whom they deem worthy. These include private clubs, private and prestigious schools and universities, certain medical facilities, and even government and governmental positions. These channels separate higher and lower classes as they offer more possibilities for contact or mingling amongst the well-to-do, increasing the probability of inter-action. They also ensure that control of the masses remains in the hands of those deemed fit by those previously appointed to further the high-born agenda.

One visual example of what the future of the world in a positive eugenics based model would look like is beautifully displayed in the movie Gattaca. Perhaps Germany, or one of the communist countries, was the example for this movie, which is a fictional depiction of a dystopian society wherein the futures of its citizens are decided based on genes. This fictional example is based in a world that uses eugenics to decide each citizen's place in that world. Those who are found to be worthy are granted elite status and privilege and access to places and situations of opportunity, and, protected by government and police - while those deemed to be low-born are denied all access and are targeted by both government and law-enforcement representatives and officials.

Negative eugenic's aim is to eliminate, through sterilization or segregation, those deemed physically, mentally, or morally "undesirable". This includes abortions, sterilization, and other methods of family planning. To note, both positive and negative eugenics can be coercive as illustrated by abortion having been encouraged for poorer, 'bad stock', while for healthy female specimens in Nazi Germany for example, abortion was illegal.

Perceived benefits of negative eugenics to its supporters involves the legal prevention of the birth of inferior human beings and was said to have begun in western European culture by the Christian Council of Adge in circa 506 AD, forbidding the marriage of cousins. In 1933, Dr. Ernst Ruedin, Hitler's director of genetics sterilization wrote that the goal of eugenicists is "to prevent the multiplication of bad stocks" and to "restrict the propagation of those physically, mentally and socially inadequate."

Furthermore, negative eugenics is seen as a human rights violation as it interferes with basic reproduction. Another inherent drawback is the loss of genetic diversity causing lower genetic variation, which results in what is known as inbreeding depression.

Even though the eugenics movement was widely criticized by many informed scholars, scientists, biologists, and authors, the Catholic Church and the Labor Party, there was still found major support from governments, private corporations and the Rich. For example, select members of the Catholic Church, which was supposedly founded upon the spirit of equality, have given millions to this organization, which was founded on the principle of in-equality.

The problem with eugenics as a whole is that its policies are governed by those in power. Let's be perfectly clear, when a government continually funds an organization practicing genocide or racism to any degree, in any form, that should be cause for alarm.

Extermination of Inferior Masses.

In the early 1930s, Nazi Germany, sought to reduce the number of those deemed 'socially inferior', which, consequently led to the extermination of millions. To be clear, Germany was said to have adopted the American eugenics model. This 'Rassenhygiene' (racial hygiene) movement was initially intended to build a 'master race' by using positive eugenics, but turned negative as the annihilation of 'inferiors' became the focus when Germany began to practice sterilization and extermination to eliminate the Jewish and other non-Aryan populations – which included blacks and mulattoes.

In the 1930s, Ernst Ruedin used eugenics as validation for the racial policies of Nazi Germany, while Adolf Hitler espoused eugenic ideas in Mein Kampf in 1925. As soon as he took power, he enacted legislation for the sterilization of what he called 'defectives', emulating what the United States had done previously. In contrast, the Nazi's Lebensborn movement spawned the creation of a foundation whose mass campaign was designed to increase the population of 'worthy' subjects. Many of these Lebensborn facilities and birth houses were created in Nazi Germany, for the sole purpose of increasing the birth rate of "Aryan" offspring from consenting or coerced extramarital relationships involving "healthy, racially pure" subjects.

The Nazi practice of euthanasia was carried out on hospital patients in the Aktion T4 centers such as Hartheim Castle. This action was taken to eliminate inferior stock and prevent their further breeding. These were in fact killing centers that began by killing the disabled, mentally disturbed and the aged, deeming them to be parasites who were not contributing to German society. This campaign eventually escalated to include the mass murder of Jews, Blacks and anyone else not deemed good enough to mix with the Aryan race. Among what was said to have been their greatest concerns were the predictability of intelligence and certain deviant behaviors.

During the Nuremberg trials, the eugenics movement became negatively associated with Nazi Germany and the Holocaust when many of the defendants attempted to justify their human rights abuses by claiming there were only minor differences between the Nazi eugenics programs and the U.S. eugenics programs. In the decades following World War II, the institution of human rights saw many countries gradually abandon eugenics policies, although some Western countries, including the United States, continued to carry out forced sterilizations.

Since the 1980s and 1990s, when new assisted reproductive technology procedures became available such as gestational surrogacy (available since 1985), preimplantation genetic diagnosis (available since 1989), and cytoplasmic transfer (first performed in 1996), fear about a possible revival of eugenics and widening of the gap between the rich and the poor has emerged.

This idea was also promoted by William Goodell (1829-1894) who advocated the castration and spaying of the insane.
Eugenics-based programs are supported by many countries. China, for example openly supports eugenics programs to the end of controlling the genetic makeup of the future. Alternatively, gene selection rather than "people selection" has recently been made possible through advances in genome editing. The moral right or wrong of these actions are determined by the ideology of the side of the fence on which you're standing.

<u>The 'Intelligence' Quotient</u>

Throughout time, there has been a movement to equate success and failure to IQ. So, it seems that the words 'criminal' and IQ tests tend to try and validate the genocide of and or eliminating certain elements as worthy of consideration for advancement. The mentally and physically challenged, members of disfavored minority groups and those who scored low in IQ test were deemed to be lesser beings and said to be unfit.

IQ Tests are also extremely biased as they are based on cultural association or subject familiarity. As before stated, true intelligence is the ability to adapt. The accumulation of knowledge makes one 'learned' not necessarily intelligent so these tests that supposedly measure intelligence should be based on one's capacity to adapt and change, not the capacity to remember. That is the issue with computers – they can store data in memory, but few have the ability to adapt. This is because the main catalyst for human change is emotion, or, energy in motion. The processing of new energy, caused by friction, brings about change in behavior. It is a fundamental property of physics. It is action-reaction. It is this adaptation that prevents computers from achieving true intelligence.

Eugenics Record Office (ERO)

In the United States, the Eugenics Record Office (ERO) was opened at Cold Spring Harbor, Long Island, N.Y., in 1910 with financial support from the legacy of railroad magnate Edward Henry Harriman. Whereas ERO efforts were officially overseen by Charles B. Davenport, (director of the Station for Experimental Study of Evolution - one of the biology research stations at Cold Spring Harbor), these ERO activities were directly superintended by Harry H. Laughlin, a professor from Kirksville, Mo. The ERO was organized around a series of missions. These missions included serving as the national repository and clearinghouse for eugenics information, compiling an index of traits in American families, training field-workers to gather data throughout the United States, supporting investigations into the inheritance patterns of particular human traits and diseases, advising on the eugenic fitness of proposed marriages, and communicating all eugenic findings through a series of publications. To accomplish these goals, further funding was secured from the Carnegie Institution of Washington, John D. Rockefeller, Jr., the Battle Creek Race Betterment Foundation (Kellogg), and the Human Betterment Foundation.

Prior to the founding of the ERO, eugenics work in the United States was overseen by a standing committee of the American Breeder's Association (eugenics section established in 1906), chaired by ichthyologist and Stanford University president David Starr Jordan. Research from around the globe was featured at three international congresses, held in 1912, 1921, and 1932. In addition, eugenics education was monitored in Britain by the English Eugenics Society (founded by Galton in 1907 as the Eugenics Education Society) and in the United States by the American Eugenics Society.

Following World War I, the United States gained status as a world power. A concomitant fear arose that if the healthy stock of the American people became diluted with socially undesirable traits, the country's political and economic strength would begin to crumble. The maintenance of world peace by fostering democracy, capitalism, and, at times, eugenics-based schemes was central to the activities of "the Internationalists," a group of prominent American leaders in business, education, publishing, and government. One core member of this group, the New York lawyer Madison Grant, aroused considerable pro-eugenic interest through his best-selling book The Passing of the Great Race (1916). Beginning in 1920, a series of congressional hearings was held to identify problems that immigrants were causing the United States. As the country's "eugenics expert," Harry Laughlin provided tabulations showing that certain immigrants, particularly those from Italy, Greece, and Eastern Europe, were significantly overrepresented in American prisons and institutions for the "feebleminded." Further data were construed to suggest that these groups were contributing too many genetically and socially inferior people. Laughlin's classification of these individuals included the feebleminded, the insane, the criminalistic, the epileptic, the inebriate, the diseased—including those with tuberculosis, leprosy, and syphilis—the blind, the deaf, the deformed, the dependent, chronic recipients of charity, paupers, and "ne'er-do-wells." Racial overtones also pervaded much of the British and American eugenics literature. In 1923, Laughlin was sent by the U.S. secretary of labor as an immigration agent to Europe to investigate the chief emigrant-exporting nations. Laughlin sought to determine the feasibility of a plan whereby every prospective immigrant would be interviewed before embarking to the United States. He provided testimony before Congress that ultimately led to a new immigration law in 1924 that severely restricted the annual immigration of individuals from countries previously claimed to have contributed excessively to the dilution of American "good stock."

Immigration control was but one method to control

eugenically the reproductive stock of a country. Laughlin appeared at the centre of other U.S. efforts to provide eugenicists greater reproductive control over the nation. He approached state legislators with a model law to control the reproduction of institutionalized populations. By 1920, two years before the publication of Laughlin's influential Eugenical Sterilization in the United States (1922), 3,200 individuals across the country were reported to have been involuntarily sterilized. That number tripled by 1929, and by 1938 more than 30,000 people were claimed to have met this fate. More than half of the states adopted Laughlin's law, with California, Virginia, and Michigan leading the sterilization campaign. Laughlin's efforts secured staunch judicial support in 1927. In the precedent-setting case of Buck v. Bell, Supreme Court Justice Oliver Wendell Holmes, Jr., upheld the Virginia statute and claimed,

*"It is better for all the world, if instead of waiting to execute degenerate offspring for crime, or to let them starve for their imbecility, society can **prevent those who are manifestly unfit from continuing their kind.**"*

Pseudoscience

After World War II, the eugenics that was once seen as science was now seen as a pseudoscience. Many scientists, physicians, and political leaders began to denounce the work of the ERO publicly. After considerable reflection, the Carnegie Institution formally closed the ERO at the end of 1939. So, even though Eugenics, due to its unpopularity was frowned upon, many organizations that practiced this art simply changed their names. For example, in 1954, Britain's 'Annals of Eugenics' renamed itself 'Annals of Human Genetics'; the 'American Eugenics Society' changed the name of its publication from 'Eugenics Quarterly' in 1969 to 'Social Biology, and, adopted the name 'Society for the Study of Social Biology' in 1972. In 1973, Edward Kennedy, whom I had the pleasure of meeting, chaired U.S. Senate hearings investigating alleged federally funded sterilization of U.S. citizens and found that thousands had been sterilized under federally supported programs. The U.S. Department of Health, Education, and Welfare proposed guidelines encouraging each state to repeal their respective sterilization laws.

Popular Support for Eugenics

During the 1930s, eugenics gained considerable popular support across the United States. Hygiene courses in public schools and eugenics courses in colleges spread eugenic-minded values to many. A eugenics exhibit titled "Pedigree-Study in Man" was featured at the Chicago World's Fair in 1933–34. Consistent with the fair's "Century of Progress" theme, stations were organized around efforts to show how favorable traits in the human population could best be perpetuated. Contrasts were drawn between the emulative, presidential Roosevelt family and the degenerate "Ishmael" family (one of several pseudonymous family names used, the rationale for which was not given). By studying the passage of ancestral traits, fairgoers were urged to adopt the progressive view that responsible individuals should pursue marriage ever mindful of eugenics principles. Booths were set up at county and state fairs promoting "fitter families" contests, and medals were awarded to eugenically sound families. Drawing again upon long-standing eugenic practices in agriculture, popular eugenic advertisements claimed it was about time that humans received the same attention in the breeding of better babies that had been given to livestock and crops for centuries.

Antieugenics Sentiment

Antieugenics sentiment began to appear after 1910 and intensified during the 1930s. Most commonly it was based on religious grounds. For example, the 1930 papal encyclical Casti Connubii condemned reproductive sterilization, though it did not specifically prohibit positive eugenic attempts to amplify the inheritance of beneficial traits. Many Protestant writings sought to reconcile age-old Christian warnings about the heritable sins of the father to pro-eugenic ideals. Indeed, most of the religion-based popular writings of the period supported positive means of improving the physical and moral makeup of humanity.

The "New Eugenics"

Applications of the Human Genome Project are often referred to as "Brave New World" genetics or the "new eugenics," in part because they have helped to dramatically increase knowledge of human genetics. In addition, 21st-century technologies such as gene editing, which can potentially be used to treat disease or to alter traits, have further renewed concerns. However, the moral, ethical, legal, and social implications of such tools are monitored much more closely than were early 20th-century eugenics programs. Appropriately, applications also generally are more focused on the reduction of genetic diseases than on improving intelligence.

Still, with or without the use of the term, many eugenics-related concerns are re-emerging as a new group of individuals decide how to regulate the application of genetics science and technology. This gene-directed activity, in attempting to improve upon nature, may not be that distant from what Galton implied in 1909 when he described eugenics as the "study of agencies, under social control, which may improve or impair" future generations.

Oh, and to be clear, a large section of the 'lessers' and 'bad stock' to whom they were referring includes blacks and minorities. The thread still goes through...

CHAPTER 10

PLANNED PARENTHOOD
OF AMERICA

In the 1980's, Planned Parenthood shifted its focus from community-based clinics to near-city minority neighborhoods.

10 PLANNED PARENTHOOD OF AMERICA

Planned Parenthood

Planned Parenthood Federation of America, Inc. (PPFA), Planned Parenthood, is a 501(c)(3), a non-profit organization providing reproductive health care in the United States and around the world. PPFA, having its roots in Brooklyn, NY, is a member of the International Planned Parenthood Federation. This is where founder Margaret Sanger opened the first birth control clinic in 1916 in the U.S. under the name The American Birth Control League. This organization, established in 1921, changed its name to Planned Parenthood in 1942.

PPFA, the largest single reproductive health services provider in the US, is also its number one provider of abortions. In 2014, PPFA's Annual Report reported seeing over 2.5 million patients in more than 4 million clinical visits and performing nearly 9.5 million services including 324,000 abortions. Including the $530 million of government funding, the annual PPFA revenue is $1.3 billion. Planned Parenthood, consisting of over 150 medical and non-medical affiliates, operates over 650 clinics in the U.S., partnering with organizations in 12 countries globally. The organization was intended to directly provide a variety of reproductive health services, including sexual education, contributing to research in reproductive technology and advocating for the protection and expansion of reproductive rights. Planned Parenthood, which may have been founded on racism or classism, is based on the belief of protecting society against 'the unfit'.

Planned Parenthood Philosophy

To understand fully the thrust of Planned Parenthood, we must look at the philosophy of its founder, Margaret Sanger. To be truthful, my research has uncovered two conflicting views associated with Sanger. Because of her associations with known racists, many have labeled her a racist. Others say she was an advocate for women, the poor and human rights. Today, Planned Parenthood vigorously supports Margaret Sanger's philosophies.

Let's examine some of her philosophy, as derived from her books and correspondence.

Margaret Sanger, Pivot of Civilization, referring to immigrants, African Americans and poor people. In this book, she called for the eradication of "...human weeds,' 'reckless breeders,' 'spawning... human beings who never should have been born." Also, "for the cessation of charity, for the segregation of morons, misfits, and maladjusted", and, for the sterilization of what she deemed "genetically inferior races." She attempts to validate her stance by arguing that attempts to assist the poor were "the surest sign that our civilization has bred, is breeding, and is perpetuating defectives, delinquents and defendants."
In this book, the chapter, "The Cruelty of Charity", she

calls medical and nursing facilities for slum mothers "insidiously injurious" inadvertently striving for ethnic cleansing or genocide. She viewed Blacks, Hispanics and Jewish immigrants as slum dwellers – whose rapid multiplication threatened to overrun the affluent – thereby contaminating them and their offspring with inferior genes.

Sanger also said "to cut down on the rapid multiplication of the unfit and undesirable at home", the nation needed to follow the country's "drastic immigration laws of 1924", during a speech at Vassar in 1926. A young Margaret Sanger, as did many of her contemporaries, spewed the same rhetoric – as revealed here by Rebecca Hagelin:

"Minorities crammed into impoverished areas in inner cities should not be having so many babies. And, of course, these minorities (including most of America's immigrants) are inferior in the human race, as are the physically and mentally handicapped. We should require mandatory sterilizations of those less desirable and promote easy access to abortion. And since sex should be a free-for-all, we must provide birth control and abortions to teenagers too. It's all for the greater good and for a more intelligent, liberated, healthier population."

To our point, it was also clear that this new movement was intended to target blacks, as well as other poor and minorities as illustrated here in a 1939 letter written to Frank Boudreau wherein she explained:

"That is not asking or suggesting competition between the intelligent and the ignorant, but a drastic curtailment of the birth rate at the source of the unfit, the diseased, and the incompetent. The birth control clinics all over the country are doing their utmost to reach the lower strata of our population".

She, Sanger is also noted to have said regarding her 1939 (Negro Project)

"We do not want word to go out that we want to exterminate the Negro population and if it ever occurs to any of their more rebellious members."

One of her counterparts, Clarence Gamble, then president of the American Eugenics Research Association, said:

"There is a great danger that we will fail because the Negroes think it a plan for extermination. Hence, let's appear to let the colored run it as we appear to let the south do the conference in Atlanta."

The result of this statement was the hiring of a full-time Negro Consultant in 1944 to lull blacks into accepting this as a positive move. The result of this action was the willing self-genocide throughout the south as the blacks readily accepted the contraceptives and abortions, guided by the 'expertise' of the Planned Parenthood representatives. This furthered Sanger's goal of eliminating "the defective and diseased elements of humanity from their reckless and irresponsible swarming and spawning."

To further illustrate her perceived racist views, we have to look at the First World Population Conference in Geneva in 1926 where she invited the foremost racists of the day including; Clarence C. Little, Edward A. East, Henry Pratt Fairchild, and Raymond Pearl. She was also active with the Ku Klux Klan, which is believed to have had a profound impact on the foundation of the eugenics movement in the early 1900's. In 1932, in the Birth Control Review, she called for greater sterilization, mandatory segregation, and rehabilitative concentration camps for all inferior stocks. In 1933, she aligned herself with Hitler's director of genetics sterilization and founder of the Nazi Society for Racial Hygiene, the previously mentioned Ernst Ruedin, publishing his article "Eugenic Sterilization: An Urgent Need, and later that year, published Leon Whitney's article entitled 'Selective Sterilization', which applauded and defended Hitler's Third Reich's racial programs.

Also, in her article 'A Plan for Peace' she wrote:

"...a stern and rigid policy of sterilization and segregation to that grade of population whose progeny is already tainted, or whose inheritance is such that objectionable traits may be transmitted to offspring."

Add this to her promotion of the "American Baby Code" wherein Sanger says America must "protect society against the propagation and increase of the unfit".

Margaret Sanger and former Planned Parenthood President Alan Guttmacher were both listed in 1956 as

members of the American Eugenics Society, Inc.
Planned Parenthood Shifts its Focus

In the 1980's, Planned Parenthood shifted its focus from community-based clinics to near-city minority neighborhoods. In the last years, it established over 100 school-based clinics nationwide, none of which are located in all-white or suburban middle-class schools. Literally all have been at Black, minority, or ethnic schools.

This trend continued into 1991. Although minorities make up only 19% of the U.S. population, 42.7% of the abortions performed by Planned Parenthood were on minorities, 23.2% of whom were African American women.

Here's the question: Did she unwittingly perpetuate the curtailment of the 'lower classes' to save them from themselves? Or, did she knowingly annihilate these 'unfits' to shield society from inferior saturation? Very much like Howard W. Campbell, it didn't matter her intention as the result is the same – the targeted eradication of 'bad stocks' and the extinguishing of the lower and unfit classes of society.

This situation is not unlike the Kurt Vonnegut's novel 'Mother Night' wherein the principle character, 'Howard W. Campbell', (secretly an American spy), becomes a well-known playwright, radio personality, and Nazi propagandist, whose propaganda actually helps strengthen the Nazi's resolve. To those watching and listening, based on his rhetoric, he was a Nazi sympathizer, when in fact he was sending coded

messages to the Allies. The company he kept and the
things he said branded him a Nazi. The same could be
said about Sanger, as she too was often in the company
of classists and the Aryan-minded. The moral of this
brilliant work is, (in Vonnegut's own words), "*We are
what we pretend to be, so, we must be careful about
what we pretend to be.*"

This correlates directly with what God told Moses; "I
Am That I Am" which to me means, 'I am as I exist' -
A human 'being' whatever I am being. In other words,
I cannot live as a proponent for freedom while
possessing slaves.

Analysis and Opinion

Planned Parenthood's mission was to have been to
serve underserved communities. Although Planned
Parenthood may not have been openly established as a
racist organization, its philosophy and deeds speak
volumes. Black financial analyst William L. Davis
argues:

*There is no way you can escape the implications,.
When an organization has a history of racism, when its
literature is openly racist, when its goals are self-
consciously racial, and when its programs invariably
revolve around race, it doesn't take an expert to realize
that the organization is indeed 'racist'. Really now,
how can anyone believe anything about Planned
Parenthood except that it is a hive of elitist bigotry,
prejudice, and bias? Just because the organization has
a smattering of minority staffers in key positions does*

nothing to dispel the plain facts.'"

Of the 80% of the facilities found in the minority neighborhoods, 35% of the women aborted are black, even though they make up only 13% of the population. In addition, abortion has reduced the black population by at least 25% since 1973. In fact, a black child is 3 to 4 times more likely to be killed in the womb than a white child in America.

This perceived inherently racist organization is the reason black babies in America are aborted three times more often than white babies and remains the number one killer of black lives in the United States. Abortion takes more black lives than HIV, heart disease, violent crime, accidents, and cancer – combined. The fact that Planned Parenthood aborts more black babies than white, only underscores the racial component found within. Although the focus is said to be on prenatal care, the majority of clinics don't provide it at all. In fact, the clinics found in inner-city neighborhoods, as well as college campuses, focus on birth control and abortions. As a matter of fact, a baby is aborted in a Planned Parenthood facility on the average of one every ninety seconds.

The truth is, even in 2007, Planned Parenthood aborted over 300,000 children. At 35% we are talking about 105,000 children. While that seems like a small portion of the 34 million blacks living in America, one must think exponentially. That 105,000 could easily translate into from 500,000 - potentially millions. In addition, the accusations of stem-cell and baby body part sales and other such indiscretions, lend themselves to questions about the ethical behavior of the organization.

This is not to say that they do no good work, as I'm sure many have benefitted from their programs. My personal stance is neither for, nor against abortion and I cast no judgement. The locations of the facilities, those who are served, and those who are impacted, are the facts that raise the questions.

A BLACK THREAD

CHAPTER II

DOMESTIC TERRORISM

Domestic terrorism is defined as terrorism that targets victims within a country by a perpetrator with the same citizenship as the victims."

11 DOMESTIC TERRORISM

Domestic Terrorism Defined

Domestic terrorism is defined as terrorism that targets victims "within a country by a perpetrator with the same citizenship as the victims." The 2001 USA Patriot Act defines Domestic Terrorism as "activities that involve acts dangerous to human life that are a violation of the criminal laws of the U.S. or of any state; or, appear to be intended to intimidate or coerce a civilian population." In 2003, the U.S. Dept. of State defined terrorism as "premeditated, politically motivated violence perpetrated against non-combatant targets by sub-national groups or clandestine agents, usually intended to influence an audience."

Some of the most horrific occurrences on American soil involved people of color. From the subjugation and torture of human beings to Jim Crow, the underlying theme of our beloved country has been racism and classism personified. From public castration, lynchings, bombings and murder, domestic terrorism has been used to create fear and establish control within indigent, as well as affluent black communities.

There have been many incidents of unarmed black men being shot by police. Statistics show that unarmed Black people in the US were more than twice as likely than unarmed white people to be killed by an officer. Members of the alleged corrupt police force of the Rampart division of the LAPD were notorious for

beating and killing unarmed minorities with impunity. They were also known for stealing drugs from police property, and, planting these drugs, and, weapons on 'suspects'. This occurred over and over again, in states all over America. In 2015 alone, there were an excess of recorded shootings of unarmed blacks all over the country. A study showed that many of these people were posing no threat at all to the officers, civilians or property. Also noteworthy is that many right-wing publications reported stories to the contrary. These truths, though they appear to be self-evident, are substantiated, or refuted by actual facts.
Just recently:

A police union requests that Amazon remove what they called an offensive 'Black Lives Matter' shirt; Trevor Noah sends cupcakes to an anti-Black Lives Matter commentator; A police officer's wife fakes a robbery and blames it on Black Lives Matter; and, Black Lives Matter creates a powerful Mannequin Challenge. How can those who, for example, fight for the rights of animals denounce the right of African Americans to say that they also matter? Shouldn't those who attack Black Lives Matter also attack PITA? In addition, here are some of these alarming and indicative statistics:

93 of the total of 990 fatal police shootings – just under 10 per cent – did not have any kind of weapon.
15 per cent of black people killed were not carrying a weapon at the time, compared to 6 per cent of whites and 11 per cent of other minority groups.
24 per cent of the black people shot dead were not

attacking anyone at the time, compared to 17 per cent of the white people and 31 per cent of non-black people from other ethnic groups.

A study based on information compiled by The Washington Post, by Dr. Justin Nix, of Louisville University, reported: "Our findings are suggestive of implicit bias – minorities were significantly more likely to have been fatally shot as a result of an apparent threat perception failure by officers." The researchers appealed to the US Government to set up an official record of police shootings, saying:

"Without more comprehensive data, we simply cannot determine whether the police disproportionately use force against minorities on a national scale." "A number of controversial shootings and deaths of black men at the hands of the police and others has sparked significant protests in the US and the Black Lives Matter campaign amid suspicions that some of the officers involved are racists. Since blacks are handled differently than other ethnicities, 'Use extreme caution' is the guidance given to most young Black men in the world when dealing with police. It is believed and highly probable that some police officers harbor explicitly biased attitudes toward minorities."

However it added:

"Psychological researchers have demonstrated that less conscious attitudes also influence police behavior."
The researchers pointed to another study, which

suggested police officers can "over time become unconsciously biased toward minorities through social conditioning". There was, they said, a "tendency to overestimate the correlation between race and crime". "In other words, the police, who are trained in the first place to be suspicious, become conditioned to view minorities with added suspicion," they wrote. The researchers suggested this could be countered by holding events attended by police officers and ordinary people, such as softball games or neighborhood block parties "which would permit officers to interact with minority citizens in an informal atmosphere" and provide officers with "direct, positive contact with citizens". They also recommended the use of cameras worn by police on their uniforms.

Previous research had shown "that officers wearing body-worn cameras were less likely to use force against citizens and less likely to have complaints filed against them than were officers not equipped with them".

In 2015 alone,
- Police killed at least 104 unarmed black people, nearly two each week.
- Nearly 1/3 of black people killed by police were identified as unarmed
- Despite black people comprising only 13% of the U.S. population, 36% of unarmed people killed by police in 2015 were black
- Unarmed black people were killed at 5x the rate of unarmed whites

Only 13 of the 104 cases where unarmed black people

were killed by police resulted in those officers being charged with a crime.

Un-Civil rights: Crimes Against Humanity

When law officials or militia from other countries kill unarmed civilians on a large scale, they are considered to have committed crimes against humanity. Why is it that when American police do the same, it is seen as justifiable homicide, even when the person shot is not aggressive, hostile or involved in any kind of criminal activity at all? This is not to say that all shootings were unjustified but when a young man's hands are handcuffed behind his back, sitting in the back of a police car, how can he fatally shoot himself.

Trevon Martin was a victim of Florida's 'Stand Your Ground' law. George Zimmerman shot and killed him for defending himself from Zimmerman's attack. The audio of the whole incident was captured on tape and Zimmerman was clearly the aggressor. After a short trail, a clearly unapologetic Zimmerman was found innocent and set free. Was this Stand Your Ground law a throwback law enacted to justify the targeting of minorities?

These 'Un-Civil Rights' activities have occurred far to often – in many forms and forums. For example: The word 'picnic' is believed to have had its origin in Oklahoma. Supposedly, every Friday, attendants of certain gatherings would randomly *'pick a nigger'* (thus, the word 'picnic') to lynch and afterwards, collect body parts as souvenirs. This was not only in

Oklahoma, but was a common practice all over America. Many say that this is folklore, but there exist far too many photos that substantiate this claim.

The late 1800's and early 1900's saw yet another such trend. Black babies were used as "gator-bait". The 'good old boys' would take, or even steal black babies from their parents, tie ropes around their necks, and set them in the Everglades and bogs at night. The incessant crying of the babies would attract the normally elusive alligators, making them easier to catch. One can only imagine the horrible fate of the innocent babies. Even though this was a normal practice during the time, commemorated with posters, buttons and plaques, this has been deemed by some to be just another Urban Legend and we are told to ignore that evidence. These stories are still told by the direct descendants of those who lived through those times.

These are just a few examples of the atrocities that were perpetrated by one race against another. The uncovering of more requires inquiring minds and a bit of diligence. I challenge you to look through the books in libraries and find what other histories await.

The 15th Amendment

History tells us that the right to vote is a privilege afforded all Americans. Voting has always been a privilege, and even a duty, for American citizens. Also, by law, no one can hinder or prevent another citizen from voting. The discrepancy lies in the interpretation of who is an American. Many immigrants and minorities, especially slaves, were not included in the definition of an American. It would take intervention from the American government to change the way blacks and minorities were seen in regard to voting rights.

The 15th Amendment to the Constitution granted the African American the right to vote in all elections. It declared that the *"right of citizens of the United States to vote shall not be denied or abridged by the United States or by any state on account of race, color or previous condition of servitude."* Although it was ratified on February 3, 1870, it took almost 100 years for it to be put into effect. The tangible and intangible barriers erected included poll taxes, bullying and coercion, and literacy tests, among other methods, found mostly in the Southern States.

One such test is this one that was given to prospective voters in Louisiana. The test was required for those chosen by the voting site stewards – at their discretion. This was a test that was given to anyone who could not prove (at the discretion of the monitor) a minimum of a fifth grade education. Many of who did in fact present this proof were still denied at the discretion of this steward. There were those of course who were grandfathered in, depending on their background or, if they were voting the 'right' way. Recently, this test was taken by Graduate and Post-Graduate students attending Harvard. These graduate students, as well as three top members of the German Bundesbank were not only unable to complete the test, as many of the questions have multiple possibilities for answers, are ambiguous, or, are just not clear. Many said that they were not able to fully understand the questions it seems that the questions were written in a way that the answers could be interpreted by the steward, so that the power of success or failure lay in his or her hands. Not one of those who took the test passed it. To top it off, ALL of these thirty ambiguous questions should have been completed in TEN minutes and ANY wrong answers would not only disqualify the testee, it also prevented them from voting again in the election. Below, you will find a copy of this test. I invite you to take it and pass it (remember that your answers can be interpreted by another at his or her discretion).

The State of Louisiana
Literacy Test (This test is to be given to anyone who cannot prove a fifth grade education.)

Do what you are told to do in each statement, nothing more, nothing less. Be careful as one wrong answer denotes failure of the test. You have 10 minutes to complete the test.

1. Draw a line around the number or letter of this sentence.

2. Draw a line under the last word in this line.

3. Cross out the longest word in this line.

4. Draw a line around the shortest word in this line.

5. Circle the first, first letter of the alphabet in this line.

6. In the space below draw three circles, one inside (engulfed by) the other.

7. Above the letter X make a small cross.

8. Draw a line through the letter below that comes earliest in the alphabet.

    Z V S B D M K I T P H C

9. Draw a line through the two letters below that come last in the alphabet.

    Z V B D M K T P H S Y C

10. In the first circle below write the last letter of the first word beginning with "L".

11. Cross out the number necessary, when making the number below one million.

    10000000000

12. Draw a line from circle 2 to circle 5 that will pass below circle 2 and above circle 4.

13. In the line below cross out each number that is more than 20 but less than 30.

    31 16 48 29 53 47 22 37 98 26 20 25

14. Draw a line under the first letter after "h" and draw a line through the second letter after "j".

abcde fghijklmnopq

15. In the space below, write the word "noise" backwards and place a dot over what would be its second letter should it have been written forward.

16. Draw a triangle with a blackened circle that overlaps only its left corner.

17. Look at the line of numbers below, and place on the blank, the number that should come next.

2 4 8 16 ____

18. Look at the line of numbers below, and place on the blank, the number that should come next.

3 6 9 ____ 15

19. Draw in the space below, a square with a triangle in it, and within that same triangle draw a circle with a black dot in it.

20. Spell backwards, forwards.

21. Print the word vote upside down, but in the correct order.

22. Place a cross over the tenth letter in this line, a line under the first space in this sentence, and circle around the last the in the second line of this sentence.

23. Draw a figure that is square in shape. Divide it in half by drawing a straight line from its northeast corner to its southwest corner, and then divide it once more by drawing a broken line from the middle of its western side to the middle of its eastern side.

24. Print a word that looks the same whether it is printed frontwards or backwards.

25. Write down on the line provided, what you read in the triangle below:

Paris
in the
the spring

26. In the third square below, write the second letter of the fourth word.

27. Write right from the left to the right as you see it spelled here.

28. Divide a vertical line in two equal parts by bisecting it with a curved horizontal line that is only straight at its spot bisection of the vertical.

29. Write every other word in this first line and print every third word in same line, (original type smaller and first line ended at comma) but capitalize the fifth word that you write.

30. Draw five circles that one common inter-locking part.

These tactics disenfranchised many African Americans and dissuaded them from voting. The majority of African Americans in the South needed the Voting Rights Act of 1965 to even be able to register to vote. Churches, the Sanctuaries

There have been many acts of terrorism in all walks of black life, many of which, included churches. Although many atrocities targeting those of color were bad, the most heinous of these crimes involved these churches. This includes fires, shootings and bombings of these perceived places of refuge. The sad part is that many of these churches were known to have people in them when they were blown up or otherwise, attacked. To top it off, many of the perpetrators were never prosecuted – although many of them were identified. I'm going to try and name all of these attacks I know, and where known, the outcomes.

1950's

Let's begin in Birmingham, Alabama and the bombing of Bethel Baptist Church Christmas Day, December 25 1956, and its attempted bombing in 1958. Less than a year later in April of 1957, during an evening service, dynamite exploded in the back of Allen Temple African Methodist Episcopal Church in Bessemer, Alabama.

1960's

In 1962, three large black churches were fire-bombed in Birmingham, Alabama on January 16. In September of that year, St. Matthew's Baptist Church of Macon, Georgia, was also burned. In one month, 5 churches were burned and in December, Bethel Baptist Church was the victim of another bombing. I'd love to stop now, but it gets worse. And here are just those that were reported. For example, in the St. James United Methodist Church and the 16th Street Baptist Church in Birmingham in 1963, twenty-two people were injured and four girls died. In June of 1964, Mount Zion Methodist Church in Longdale, Mississippi, was burned to the ground. The 16th Street Baptist Church bombing was said to have been an act of white supremacist terrorism which occurred in Birmingham, Alabama on Sunday, September 15, 1963. Four members of the Klu Klux Klan planted more than 15 sticks of dynamite with a timing device on the east side of the church, beneath the steps. Keep in mind that murder was the intention as they knew that on Sunday morning, many men, women and children would be unsuspectingly in attendance.

Even more shocking was the fact that even though the FBI knew who perpetrated the crime, it took them between 14 and 37 years to convict them. One person even passed away in 1994 before his trial, so he was never charged with his alleged involvement in the bombing.

1970's

In 1972, in Reston, Virginia Cartersville Baptist Church was burned, causing its main church to crash into the basement. A short time later, in 1974 Edward

Boykin, as well as Alberta King, mother of Martin Luther King were killed in Ebenezer Baptist Church in Atlanta, Georgia. The man who killed them and wounded another just decided that "Black ministers were a menace to Black people". Second Wilson Church of Chester, South Carolina was gutted by fire in December of 1979.

1990's

Like today, the apple doesn't fall far from the tree. In Pike County Mississippi, April 1993, three teens are convicted and served time for setting fire to Rocky Point Missionary Baptist Church. Many of the perpetrators of these terrorist acts had strong or family ties to the Ku Klux Klan. As with the 'amendments' to the U.S. Constitution, Congress finally had to pass the 'Church Arson Prevention Act' as a result of more than 30 churches being burned during an 18 month period in 1995-96.

2000's

One would think that this type of mindless, barbaric, Neanderthalic activity would have ended in the new millennium, but it continues well into the 21st century. Let's fast-forward to 2006 in Richmond, Virginia where a cross was burned outside a black church. I guess the cross is not as sacred as the flag to some. In 2008 and 2010, Klan members and want-to-be's left calling cards in the forms of racist, threatening graffiti and fire bombings in Springfield, Massachusetts and Crane, Texas. These perpetrators we caught and sentenced.

In **2014**, the killing of Michael Brown Jr., one of the many questionable police shootings of black men, (as mentioned before, most of whom were unarmed), prompted a series of protests at Flood Christian Church in Ferguson, Missouri. Whether the church was burned in retaliation to comments made by the pastor regarding the release of the officer who shot Brown, or in response to the protests, it was an atrocious act that caused the burning of several other buildings in the area as well, threatening the lives of men, women and children.

2015 was filled with incidents in North and South Carolinas, Tennessee and Georgia as Blacks were murdered and churches were burned and bombed. Even more recently, in 2016, Hopewell Missionary Baptist Church in Greenville, Mississippi was burned and vandalized with graffiti. The words "Vote Trump" was spray-painted on the building intended to be voting intimidation. In all fairness, the arsonist was said to have been a black member of the church.

These are just some of the examples of domestic terrorism of which we speak. Add to that armed retaliation to peaceful protests, the violent enforcement of Jim Crow, creative forms of genocide, and multiple shootings of unarmed blacks by police officers with no retribution or accountability, and a pattern definitely appears.

Many articles and films like 'Birth of a Nation' created

a completely skewed narrative about Blacks and Black life. It showed Blacks as evil, lazy, dumb, sneaky and dangerous. The most important issue with this movie is that the ones portraying the 'evil black men' were whites in 'Blackface'.

In like kind, quite a few movies seem to have hidden agendas including 'Lord of the Rings' and many of the action hero movies that have been made. Why is it that ordinary people, most of whom are clearly of European descent, are to overcome the 'dark forces' in so many films? Is this a form of subconsciously programming people to see dark faces as threatening while programming our brains to see lighter skin as heroes and saviors? I've often wondered why most minions are dark, shadowy figures.

Without proper education, almost anyone would be ignorant of possibilities and procedure. Motivation is usually guided by hope and possibility. Taking away all hope and eliminating possibilities lead to stagnation.

Black Wall Street: A Nation Unto Itself

The terrorist attack on the federal building in Oklahoma City, Oklahoma is said to have been the most devastating attack to have occurred on American soil. This could not be further from the truth.

In 1921, almost 100 years ago, in the same state, an even deadlier attack occurred - with more suspected casualties. Keep in mind that this is not to disrespect any of the casualties of the OKC bombing, or their families, just an acknowledgement of seemingly overlooked facts. It seems as though the media has overlooked this attack as significant altogether.

Black Wall Street in Tulsa, Oklahoma was the place wherein international business flourished from the early 1900's until June 1, 1921. That's when the largest massacre of non-military Americans in the history of this country took place, led by the Ku Klux Klan. On this date, Black Wall Street was bombed from the air and burned to the ground by mobs of envious whites.
This Tulsa race riot occurred when a white mob began attacking residents and businesses in the affluent Greenwood community in Tulsa, Oklahoma. This, one of the most heinous racial crimes in U.S. history, was said to have been started in response to the raping of a white elevator attendant by a young Black man in a commercial building over the memorial weekend. Add to that McDade, a Black treasurer from Kansas, being elected by the citizens of the state, and the Ku Klux Klan openly saying that they would kill him within 48 hours if he took office. As a direct result of these occurrences, perceived or legitimate, the indigenous whites of the area responded with brutal, relentless force. This attack was carried out on the ground and by air, devastating at least 35 blocks of the district, which, at that time, was the wealthiest Black community in the nation.

Black Wall Street, or 'Little Africa' (as it was known), located in Greenwood, Tulsa, Oklahoma could have been the poster-child for the way Black communities were run at that time. Its isolated location was one of over 28 Black townships located in Oklahoma, as it was set aside as a Black and Indian state. Between 1830 and 1832, at least a third of the people who travelled with AmerIndians along the 'Trail of Tears' were Black.

During this time, many Blacks and Amerindians owned land, which was found to have possessed oil. This made these communities wealthy and prosperous. In addition, because of Jim Crow laws and segregation, they did most of their business with, and depended on, each other. For example, if a tragedy occurred in one of these neighborhoods, the citizens would band together to resolve it as quickly as possible. Many Blacks intermarried into Amerindian culture and cultivated the oil found on their '40 acres and a mule'.

This resulted in a most affluent, self-sufficient community whose thrust was education and economic stability. This translated into a thriving infrastructure. Ron Wallace, a Tulsa native, and Jay Wilson of Los Angeles, reported that at that time, "The dollar circulated 36 to 100 times, sometimes taking a year for currency to leave the community." Today, a dollar leaves the Black community in less than 15-minutes."
Was this seen as a pre-Keynesian, Neo-liberalistic society due to its exclusion of outside influences? Many of its attributes including free trade, the increased role of the private sector in its economy, politics and society, self-sufficiency and privatization, echo the characteristics of neo-liberalism and

therefore, possibly posed a threat to the status quo.
The main thoroughfare was Greenwood Avenue which
was intersected by Archer and Pine Streets. From the
first letters in each of those three names, Greenwood,
Archer and Pine, you get G.A.P., and that's where the
renowned R & B music group the *Gap Band* got its
name. They're from Tulsa.

During the 1900's, this 'gateway to the black
community' was nationally famous for many things.
The area's 600 businesses and 36 square blocks with
the population of 15,000 African Americans enraged
the lower-economic Europeans, as they really believed
in, and practiced nepotism. The typical family then
was five children or more, though the typical farm
family would have 10 kids or more who made up the
nucleus of the labor. Abraham Lincoln said "Teach the
children, so it will not be necessary to teach the
adults." The focus on the future of the community was
to properly educate every child. For example, the
average student went to school on Black Wallstreet in
a suit and tie because of the morals and respect they
were taught at a young age. Downright Ivy League!
Many learned and accomplished Ph.D.'s also lived and
prospered in Little Africa, both Black attorneys and
doctors. At that time, physicians even owned medical
schools. One doctor was Dr. Berry who owned the bus
system, and whose average income was $500 a day in
1910. There were also pawn shops everywhere,
brothels, jewelry stores, 21 churches, 21 restaurants
and two movie theaters. During that time, the entire
state of Oklahoma had only two airports, yet six
Blacks owned their own planes.

To illustrate just how affluent many of these Blacks were, they were able to do things most Whites at the time could only dream of. One such example was the wife of a banker named California Taylor in the neighboring town, whose father also just happened to own the largest cotton gin west of the Mississippi. California was so well-off that every three months, she would take a cruise to Paris, France, just to have her clothes made. Two highly successful brothers in nearby Wagner County, one with a large spinach farm, and the other with a large potato farm, would each fill 100 boxcars per day.

Riots & History Lost

"The Tulsa race riot of 1921 was hidden from history books, classrooms or even in private. Blacks and whites alike grew into middle age unaware of what had taken place." Here is the billion-dollar question, why was this tragedy excluded from history?
Searching under the heading of "riots", "Oklahoma" and "Tulsa" in current editions of the World Book Encyclopedia, there is conspicuously no mention whatsoever of the Tulsa race riot of 1921, and this omission is by no means a surprise, or a rare case. The fact is, one would also be hard-pressed to find documentation of the incident, let alone an accurate accounting of it, in any other "scholarly" reference or American history book.
That's precisely the point that noted author, publisher and orator Ron Wallace, a Tulsa native, sought to make nearly five years ago when he began researching

this riot, one of the worst incidents of violence ever visited upon people of African and Amerindian descent. Ultimately joined on the project by colleague Jay Wilson of Los Angeles, the duo found and compiled indisputable evidence of what they now describe as "a Black holocaust in America."

In their self-published book, *Black Wall Street: A Lost Dream,* and its companion video documentary, Black Wall Street: A Black Holocaust in America!, the authors have chronicled for the very first time in the words of area historians and elderly survivors what really happened there on that fateful summer day in 1921 and why it happened. Wallace similarly explained why this bloody event from the turn of the century seems to have had a recurring effect that is being felt in predominately Black neighborhoods even to this day.

Survivors interviewed say that they think that the whole thing was planned because during the time that all of this was going on, white families with their children stood around the borders of their community and watched the massacre, the looting and everything-- much in the same manner they would watch a lynching.

The attack was said to have been initiated by the KKK in conjunction with high-ranking city officials, the police and National Guard, and other sympathizers. The same Ku Klux Klan that agued the genetic inferiority of Blacks and other minorities were jealous of their success and sought to destroy this shining example of what they were able to accomplish. This successful community only disproved Margaret

Sanger's 'inferior genes' theory, as it took intelligence, hard work and tenacity to establish, and then, maintain such an environment. To be clear, these are the qualities Sanger, her counterparts, and the KKK said the minorities did not possess.
This seems to be the way a white-centric regime chooses to handle mass Black success – destroy it, so as not to allow heroes to emerge. The question is, was this the reason for the attack?

Here is where the facts get dodgy. One report said that more than 800 people were admitted to hospitals, and, even though they were the ones who had been attacked, more than 6,000 Black residents were arrested and detained, many for several days. The Oklahoma Bureau of Vital Statistics officially recorded 39 dead, where the American Red Cross said it was about 300, the number historians agree upon.

After the aforementioned accused young Black man had been taken into custody, it was rumored throughout the Black community that he was about to be lynched - a common response to any allegations against Blacks at the time. So, exercising their second amendment rights, they showed up at the police station in armed protest, which was not well received by the White mob that had already gathered there. What happened next is the natural course of angry people with guns and purpose – chaos! A confrontation ensued, shots were fired, and some whites and blacks were killed.

As the news of this skirmish spread throughout the city, mob violence exploded. Thousands of whites stormed through this black community that night and the next day, killing men, women, and children, burning and looting stores and homes. About 10,000 black people were left homeless, and property damage surpassed $1.5 million in real estate, as well as $750,000 in personal property (well over $30 million in 2017). Eye witnesses said that both the police and National Guard joined the looting mob, firing automatic weapons into the Black homes and businesses, while airplanes dropped sticks of dynamite on the Black community as well. In an eyewitness account discovered in 2015, Greenwood attorney Buck Colbert Franklin described watching a dozen or more planes using military force, which, had been dispatched by the city police force, drop burning balls of turpentine on Greenwood's rooftops.

During this period of less than 12 hours, this once thriving Black business district in northern Tulsa lay demolished and smoldering. Imagine, a model community devastated, and a major African-American economic movement resoundingly defused.

The attack resulted in the deaths of over 300 African-Americans and Amerindians, as well as over 600 prominent businesses destroyed. Included in these were the 21 restaurants, 2 movie theaters, 21 churches, 30 grocery stores, plus a bank, a post office, a hospital, libraries, schools, law offices, a bus system, and 6 private planes.

There was an effort toward public education about these events through the process. The Commission's final report published in 2001 said that the city had conspired with the white mob against the Tulsa black community; it recommended a program of reparations to survivors and their descendants. The state passed legislation to establish some scholarships for descendants of survivors, encourage economic development of Greenwood, and develop a memorial park in Tulsa to the riot victims. The park was dedicated in 2010.

Philadelphia Bombing

Police in Philadelphia also bombed a neighborhood in 1985 because they were using their first Amendment right of free speech using a bullhorn. Neighbors also complained that their 'back to nature' lifestyle was attracting pests. The reason given for the bombing was that the radical black liberation group 'MOVE' had been using a west Philadelphia row house as a commune since 1981. On May 13, 1985, police bombed a building said to contain indicted MOVE members. After bombing a suspected bunker from a helicopter, the building caught on fire, spreading throughout the neighborhood to another 65 or so houses. Sources say the fire department was ordered not to put the fires out.

A BLACK THREAD

CHAPTER 12

SPORTS

The Black athlete is said to be in many cases,
physically superior but mentally inferior to other races

12 SPORTS

Racism in Sports

Sports, as with many social functions involving different ethnicities, are microcosms of larger social make-ups. The issue of racism in sports is something people in America, and around the world it seems, would rather ignore.

The Black athlete is said to be in many cases, physically superior but mentally inferior to other races. Many postulate that physical prowess is closely linked to animalistic characteristics and that this sort of primal anti-intellectualism is what makes blacks better at running and jumping. For example, some say that mega athletes like LeBron James are becoming the wrong types of role models because they promote physical abilities as opposed to intellectual development. It is believed that these types of heroes do more damage than not to the black communities as it stunts economic growth. What is not mentioned in that same light is that James is not only physically gifted, but also has one of the world's highest basketball IQ's.

Even though sports point directly to the mental and physical abilities of the participants, there are certain who would shackle some of those superior athletes so as to give the appearance of equality. On many occasions, the rules are bent or certain potential participants barred from even competing to prevent revealing the existence of a physical imbalance.

Here is the secret: Melanin, or Carbon. It is a fact that carbon processes energy more effectively – amplifying it if you will. This is evident in the fuels we use to magnify energy sources. We burn oil and coal to radiate heat. While many of you will call this folly, the ancients knew what we choose to ignore.

Opinions Revealed

On the 40th anniversary of Jackie Robinson's admission into the majors, Al Campanis, former Los Angeles Dodger Vice President for player personnel (arguably one of baseball's fairest, more equal-opportunity employers) was interviewed by Ted Koppel on the American investigative TV program, ABC's Nightline. When asked his opinion of why there were so few blacks in management in major league baseball, he replied, "*I truly believe they (blacks) may not have some of the necessities to be a field manager or perhaps a general manager*". He went on to say that blacks aren't adapted to be swimmers because they lack buoyancy.

Baseball's first black manager, Frank Robinson, when asked about Campanis said that he was a decent man who was just a product of baseball's traditional thinking - "*... that blacks aren't smart enough to be managers or third-base coaches or part of the front office. There's a belief that they're fine when it comes to the physical part of the game, but if it involves brains they just can't handle it*".

On the other side, former CBS sportscaster Jimmy "the Greek" Snyder said in January of 1988, that heredity was the reason blacks are better athletes than whites because

"This all goes back to the Civil War, when during the slave trade, the slave owner would breed his big black to his big woman so that he could have a big black kid. That's where it all started."

The words that seemed to anger his white counterparts most were his statements about blacks' athletic advantage being a result of them having bigger thighs. He also received backlash for having stated:

"They've got everything. If they take over coaching like everybody wants them to, there's not going to be anything left for the white people. I mean all the players are black. The only thing the whites control are the coaching jobs"

This statement, although it seemed racist, was actually reverse racism and served to disprove the claims of staunch racists. His words suggest that due to heredity and lifestyle, namely slavery, blacks were physically superior and that whites were lazy and as a result, not willing to put in the necessary work it takes to get better. He also pointed out that blacks consistently put in the work it takes to become better athletes.

A truism is that people normally reach for that which is within their grasp. If I believe or am told that I can accomplish a thing, then I may at least try to do it –

and vice-versa. 'You can't' is often as powerful as 'I can'. Many of these beliefs and attitudes are handed down from generation to generation inspiring or inhibiting the receiver's development. It is the error of knowing the unknown, trusting in the source of the information so much that even without proof, it is seen, felt and acted upon. This is the same ignorance that fosters prejudice, the only cure for which is knowledge.

Let's examine the numbers. Although blacks make up approximately 13% of the American population, they comprise the largest percentages of the most physical sports. In fact Black athletes constitute approximately 75% of the NBA, 70% of the WNBA and 68.5% of the NFL.

Whenever blacks have managed to achieve a certain level of success in a given realm, be it sports, politics or whatever, the rules or criterion have been subsequently or mysteriously altered so as to deter or bar further black advancement.

For centuries, whites have exerted physical dominance over what they considered to be inferior blacks. They beat, raped, castrated, lynched and worse, with impunity. These blacks were told that they were worthless, or in the least, worth less. This mindset continued throughout the 20th century, well into the 21st century. Even though biologically there is a noticeable difference between blacks and whites, there is still the nature v's nurture argument.

Black kids grow up being told that they are physically

and mentally inferior. Many are denied the proper training that those of other races enjoy through access and privilege. This is what I believe to be the driving force behind black athletic achievement and physical superiority. Form a place of comfort one can be relaxed, cold and calculating (as calculations take time). So, to say that whites are more intelligent is quite the misnomer. They've just had more free time to plan and prepare. Black athletes play with the aggression of retaliation for having been mistreated and bullied.

In the modern era, the way sports are perceived and handled, reveal a disparity in the way different colors of athletes are also handled. As previously mentioned, sports are seen as at least one microcosm of social structure and even encompasses military strategies.
From Jack Jones and Jesse Owens, to Ezekiel Elliott and Colin Kaepernick, men of certain ethnicities and social stature decided that those of other colors were physically or psychologically inferior to compete with white athletes. This led to redefining existing rules and regulations or just changing them altogether to level the actual or proverbial playing fields. Although this is true in baseball, boxing, golf, tennis, basketball, polo, auto-racing and many other sports, we will examine just a few. We will examine the reasons for some of the arbitrary rules and regulations in these sports, as well as the affect these rules had on the black athletes who overcame them.

Bicycle Racing

In the 1890's, at a time before automobiles, bicycling was one of the most popular and exciting sports in America. It is said to have been more popular than baseball or boxing. During this time in American history, this too was segregated, as Blacks were not allowed to compete professionally.

In Indianapolis, Indiana, 17-year old Marshall Taylor set out to break the cycling color line. A newspaper delivery person, he used his bike in his work. In between that, he would pedal as fast as he could, training himself for an opportunity that seemed light years away. He believed that his one-mile sprints were some of the fastest in the world at the time and he just needed a chance to prove it. But, all seemed hopeless as the sport did not allow blacks.

1896 in Indianapolis would provide a perfect, but dangerous opportunity for the 17-year old stallworth Taylor. The race, sponsored by 'The League of American Wheelmen' was to have an uninvited guest. He rode onto the track in between races and began to circle the track. To the amazement of shocked onlookers, he unofficially shattered the indoor world record by 8 seconds. Over the next 10 years, he wins over half the races in which he competes and holds 7 world records.

Baseball

Blacks were kept out of the American and National

Baseball Leagues because they were said to have been inferior, even though they were doing amazing things in the 'Negro League'. They were doing super-human things with balls and bats but were said to have been inferior.

The rule that kept Blacks out of baseball was called a "Gentlsman's Agreement." This in itself has major significance when one understands what the word gentleman means.

Gentleman: *Gentle, root-gentil comes from Old French meaning 'high born, noble, of good family+man, comes from Old English, hence the word literally means "well-born- man". any man above the social rank of a yeoman, including the nobility.*

So, in a sense, the rule inferred that if one was not well-born, or had been perceived to have been devoid of social grace, or of noble birth, he would not be allowed to play. This rule, along with others like it, made sure that blacks would not be allowed to play baseball in the major leagues - and they didn't until 1945-46.

Other than a few exceptions, black were kept out of baseball and the minor leagues from its inception until 1947. The gentlemen had an oral agreement that those of African descent would not be allowed entry to organized baseball in the majors or the minors. Mind you, there were at least a couple of blacks playing the sport pre-1887, but the high minor league's vote in 1887 barred new contracts with black players anywhere in organized baseball in the major leagues and the high and low minors. During this time however, a few light-skinned black, Hispanics, native Hawaiians and Amerindians were allowed to play on some teams, but their ethnicities were kept on the down low so as not to infuriate patrons.

This color line was in full effect until the admission of Jackie Robinson with the Brooklyn Dodgers who entered the league in 1946-47. Both he and Larry Doby, who played for the Cleveland Indians, would have to represent a race previously said not to have been good enough to be allowed to play the sport.
Although there are a number of blacks and minorities playing the sport today, their numbers in the game itself, as well as management, are still grossly under-represented. Add to that the racial taunting of minorities in as late as 2017, not unlike the player and fan hazing of Jackie Robinson, and one can see how far the sport has to go to be equal.

Boxing

Boxing or pugilism has been called the sport of kings. In Ancient Greece, and long before, boxing was considered an amateur competitive sport and was also included in the first Olympic Games. Also, in Rome, boxers were believed to have worn the 'Cestus' – hand coverings with metal studs often used to maim, mutilate or even kill their opponents. Many of them were a welcome addition to the Roman gladiatorial spectacle. The revival of the 'sport' occurred in London as bare-knuckle competition. In these 'prize-fights', the contestants fought for money as on-lookers bet on the outcomes.

In a 2012 radio interview, former Heavyweight Champion, Mike Tyson exposes some little known truths about boxing. He says Jim Bleacher set up the sport to minimize the casualties of Irish and Dutch gang wars. The red and blue colors in the corners initially represented the gangs to which the fighters belonged. These colors also carried political significance – i.e., republicans and democrats. The sport pitted the strongest of one gang against the strongest of the other. The winner would decide how territories and wealth would be divided until the next fight.

The first recognized Heavyweight Champion was James Figg in 1719. Later, in 1743, John Broughton civilized the sport with rules that eliminated the then normal practices of hitting opponents when they were down, pulling hair, putting foreign substances in the eyes, and biting. It wasn't until 1838 that Broughton's rules were adopted into the Original London Prize Ring Rules, which lasted until the 'Marquis of Queensberry Rules' of 1857.

These 'Queensberry Rules' would focus on the use of hands and finesse as opposed to tussling, agility and brute strength. They would establish the guide by which today's boxing is governed, with gloves and timed intervals inside a ring. Although the last sanctioned bare-knuckled fight involving John L. Sullivan was fought in 1889, there was still a desire for the knock-down, drag out fights that made the sport so popular. Enter the 'Battle Royale', the unsanctioned practice of pitting poor black youth and men against one another for money or food. They were rounded up and made to fight each other for the amusement and waging of white spectators. While many of these combatants faded away into obscurity, at least one would rise to become legend. His name was Jack Johnson.

During my research, I found that many white writers refer to the white fighters of antiquity in the highest regard with names such as 'The Honorable', 'The Great...' or 'Gentleman...', while giving blacks less flattering monikers.

Jack Johnson was the first recognized black Heavyweight Champion. The first African American pop icon, his reign lasted from 1908 to 1915. He was so popular that he was photographed and written about more than anyone else of his day – black or white. It is safe to say that he was the Michael Jackson of that time, steeped in admiration and controversy alike. Although he was only an athlete, he received much more attention than then president of the Tuskegee Institute Booker T. Washington, founder of the N.A.A.C.P., W.E.B. Du Bois, actors George and Bert Walker, or even Scott Joplin, combined.

He lived his life like a rock star and was actually scrutinized as such. As sports became an important aspect of the American cultural and social landscape, the position he held became more and more significant. This phenomenon was due to boxing being the most filmed sport of the day and even being shown in movie theaters. Add to that his association with the newest innovation, the Automobile, and his passion for what we now know as driving, which placed him in an elite strata, only dreamed about by common people.

Prior to Johnson's ascent, there existed at least two well-known black Heavyweights from the bare-knuckle era. These were ex-slaves Bill Richmond and Tom Molyneaux from England whose prowess and savvy in the ring afforded them major success. This was during a time when wrestling and pummeling were still allowed and favored in the sport.

Aside from being juicy tidbits of history, why is this significant? It is significant because during this time, many other sports which include football, baseball, basketball and virtually all other sports had provisions that prohibited, or limited black participation. Boxing was one of the only sports that allowed black participation - primarily against each other.

Even though blacks had proven that they could excel in the sport having many champions including: Joe Walcott- Welterweight Champion form 1901-1904; Joe Gans – Lightweight Champion from 1902-1904 and 1906-1908; and, George Dixon- Featherweight Champ from 1890-1897 and 1898-1900, as well as Bantamweight Champion from 1890-1892, they were still not allowed to compete for the most coveted Heavyweight crown.

It is important to note that the pivotal 1896 Supreme Court decision of Pressy v's Ferguson, which stated that Jim Crow laws were not unconstitutional, accommodated state-sponsored segregation allowing the legal exclusion of blacks and minorities. from participating with the ' imperial' Anglo-Saxon race. The advent of post-Civil War 'Social Darwinism' became a banner for white America who believed themselves to be the master-race and that all others were mentally and physically inferior.

As a result, no Heavyweight from John Sullivan to Jim Jefferies would even consider allowing a black man to contend for the Heavyweight crown, even though there were many blacks who were more than qualified. These include: Petyr Jackson, Sam McVey, Sam Langford, Denver Ed Martin and Joe Jeanette. Just like baseball, jockeying, football, and many other sports of the time, blacks were excluded or at least 'grandfathered out'. (That means, if your grandfather was a slave, you couldn't participate). Often when mixed fights did occur, the white boxer was declared the winner despite the actual winner, and many cases ended up 'non-decisions'.

Johnson Overcomes

Education, intelligence and the will to succeed appear to have been what drove the 6ft, 200 lb Johnson and kept him on his path to greatness. He was surrounded by mediocrity and was frequently told that his reach exceeded his grasp. Learning to read and write, he became more informed than most of his contemporaries. So, while they were content to work the available labor jobs, he saw something more – living by the code that it is better to work smart, than to work hard. However, at the time, his sport was surrounded by pimps, whores, drugs, shady management and illegally fixed fights.

His focus allowed him to avoid the common pitfalls of his new-found profession which included alcoholism, crime, drug-addiction and venereal disease, common for the day. His intelligence drove him to train and save his money while most of his contemporaries, having been deprived of living freely, began to do so, exhausting their purses – often to their own demise.

During Johnson's meteoric rise, Jim Jeffries retired and a new champion, Tommy Burns emerged. After having risen through the ranks, Johnson was at first denied a chance at the title by Burns. This decision echoed the consensus of most whites in America at the time. Although, the majority of whites felt that no black man should contend for the coveted Heavyweight title, there were a few very influential persons who disagreed with that sentiment. These included the publisher of the Police Gazette, most popular newspaper of the day, Richard K. Fox.

After succumbing to Burn's outrageous demands, the fight finally took place on December 26, 1908, which Johnson won easily. In desperate hope of neutralizing Johnson, they asked that Jim Jeffries come out of retirement. Jeffries had never been beaten and many still considered him to be the champion. The fight, seen to many as a mini race war, took place in Reno,

Nevada on July 4, 1910. Johnson won again easily, taunting and playing with Jeffries, which infuriated many whites. Jeffries was known to have said that although he was one of the best fighters of the day, he did not possess the strength or skill to have beaten Johnson.

Add to that acknowledgement of defeat Johnson's bragging and taunting opponents in the ring, and it becomes quite clear why he was among the most hated by whites. This type of taunting and bragging was commonplace within the boxing community but coming from a black man who should know his place, it was unheard of.

Johnson's Habits

In addition, he was dating, having sexual relations with, as well as marrying white women, something that at the time, was frowned upon by whites and blacks alike. It affected whites because they felt that he sullied their 'kind', and blacks because they feared the wrath and backlash of retribution for his actions. After Johnson's win and the unsuccessful placement of the 'great white hope', the sitting gentry sought to defeat Johnson with precedent and jurisdiction. I've always felt that Johnson's wins were the catalyst in the making of the controversial 'Birth of a Nation', but that's just my own speculation from here in the future.

In many, many cases, the narrative doesn't agree with the facts. Many white men of the time were not the paragons of virtue they appeared to be or even said they were. In theory, they were the pillars of morality who stood for truth, justice and the American way. The truth was far less flattering. The Reconstruction Era offered the unscrupulous an open window of opportunity to make gains previously relegated to a select few. From 'carpetbagging' to sharecropping, many of these men found their way into the political arena as participants or backers through which they could actually create and/or impact laws and legislation.

Such legislation would be the undoing of Johnson and topple his reign, crucifying him in the court of public opinion.

The early 1900's saw 4 amendments to the constitution in addition to the 'Mann Act', which sought to minimize prostitution- specifically inter-state prostitution. The propaganda of the time warned of Asian sex rings that lured innocent white women into opium dens and sold them or their bodies across state lines. The Mann Act prohibited inter-state prostitution and was in direct response to innocent white women being supposedly corrupted by untrustworthy minorities. The point is that these innocents were just as likely to have been corrupted by unscrupulous white men, knowing they could just blame the minorities. During this tumultuous time of American rebirth, immorality, and the causes of it in any form, became a target. With Jazz music from black musicians, alcohol from speak-easy's and after-hour joints, the Asian opium invasion, and Women's Rights, it was easy for politicians and the media to tie immoral behavior to race mixing.

The suicide of Johnson's first wife, Etta Duryea, raised suspicion over him as he was always with a wife and a concubine – who was usually a prostitute – in this case, Lucille Cameron. To the horror of white America, three months after the death of his wife, he married Cameron to counter the federal case being built against him using the Mann Act, as a wife cannot testify against her husband. Already convicted in the court of public opinion, pressure was on the government to find a witness for a Mann Act violation tied to Johnson who, with his boxing, nightclubs and open sexuality, was a moral time bomb. They actually found what they were looking for in Belle Schreiber, a prostitute with whom Johnson had an ongoing affair. He took her with him from state to state which was the Mann Act violation for which they searched, and with which they prosecuted him. Even though the Mann Act was a bad law and folly at best, they used it to successfully prosecute Johnson so as to topple the giant he had become to appease the masses. Just like today's justice system, he was given the maximum sentence for a minor offense.

The result of which was the return of the title to the white race. For the next 22 years, blacks were denied a shot at the title and wouldn't be allowed to even compete for it until Joe Louis in 1937.

This is just one of the examples of how the changes in the rules and regulations of the sport of boxing were at the expense of Blacks. The stories of Muhammad Ali and Mike Tyson are equally as interesting.

Basketball

Basketball is yet another sport wherein the rules were changed as a result of black physical dominance. Whether it was due to viewer decline, white players getting humiliated, or just to soften up the game, the rules took the balance of power away from those who controlled it with physical prowess and returned it to a time when blacks were not allowed to even play. The distance shot, the moving of the basketball 'around the horn' are phrases of a game that was played pre-black players. If one doesn't believe me, just watch a game from the 1940's or 1950's. They will look eerily similar to the style of play we see emerging today.

An early example of changing the rules to level the field has to do with the 'Lou Alcindor Rule'. Due to the dominance and athleticism of Black basketball players from the year 1967 to 1976, 'dunking' was prohibited in the NCAA (National College Athletic Association). Players such as Kareem Abdul Jabbar (Lou Alcindor) were so dominant that the rules had to be changed so as to prevent other players from being totally humiliated. Dunking was prohibited because blacks such as Alcindor had an unfair advantage.

As a result of black dominance of the sport, the '3 point shot' was instituted, as whites were equal to, if not better than, blacks at long-range sniping. The spin is that it was added to speed up the game. That's why the play of the Golden State Warriors with three-point masters Steph Curry and Clay Thompson is so important. It is the realization of the shift from black dominated 'power-ball', to the more complacent 'chucker-ball' of the by-gone era. The announcers even say, (unbeknownst to the normal public), that the sport has been waiting for this shift. They've taken the aggression out of the game and made it lily-passive. The powers that be have even found a way to discredit the physical abilities and accomplishments in favor of intention. In other words, 'analytics' hold the studying and taking of the test in higher esteem then the results or 'the eyeball test'. Sentences such as "he may not have won but let's give him equal credit for having played better" are the words we now hear. The issue is that this data is what history will remember as it is the written account of what 'happened'.. So now, analytics are what performance is based upon, not the athleticism of an athletic sport.

Allen Iverson

In many cases, the usage of trumped-up charges, or just flat-out lies have been used to level the proverbial playing field. The villainization of prominent athletes is a tool used to eliminate heroes. In the case of the great basketball guard Allen Iverson, this could not have been more glaring. In his junior year at Bethel High School, he blossomed into a two-sport star. From the hardwood to the gridiron, he set records and a winning pace and, displayed phenomenal leadership potential. Winning the Virginia State Championship in football, and basketball, and being named both football and basketball player of the year in 1993, he was on his way to stardom. Ranked No. 1 of all 125 college prospects, every college had an interest in the star athlete. However, due to being in the wrong place at the wrong time, he was accused by members and associates of a rival team of something that could have derailed him forever.

Racial tensions were already high as a result of the Rodney King verdict and Virginia is well-known as a hotbed of race-related activity. The brawl broke out in a bowling alley when members of a rival school pelted Iverson with racial slurs (believed to have come from jealousy over his recent successes) and Iverson's companions rose to his defense.

In this brawl involving several people, Iverson was alleged to have smashed a chair on a woman and consequently convicted of 'maiming by mob' (a federal offense) and sentenced to a 15-year prison term. It was clear that the skirmish involved violence from members of both sides of the racially charged incident but ironically, Iverson and three of his Black companions were the only one's arrested in the altercation. Thankfully, it was overturned four months later by the Governor due to insufficient evidence and he was set free, but the damage had already been done. This was another clear case of 'sending a message' that you all had better get in line.

This verdict was clearly hate-related and a bending of the laws and rules again. I personally see a correlation to the acquittals of the officers involved in the 1992 Rodney King beating. Was Iverson a victim of a media misdirect designed to create a balance? It is clear to see however, that once labeled by the powerful system, those labels follow you for a lifetime.

Track and Field

In 1908, John Taylor, a freshman at the University of
Pennsylvania, was the first black to win an Olympic
gold medal. He won it as a member of the US relay
team. We also recognize 1936 gold medalist, Jesse
Owens. Upon winning the 200 meter dash decisively,
and setting a new Olympic record, Jesse Owens
attempted to shake Hitler's hand. It was refused and
the American media echoed its outrage. Even though
during this time, because of Jim Crow, many
American whites handled blacks the same way.

Most of the Olympic medals won by blacks throughout
time were in track and field and boxing. The
phenomenal Olympic successes of Cullen Andrew
Jones and Simone Manuel in swimming may have
come much sooner had blacks not been prohibited
from swimming pools and discouraged from even
competing in the sport. It was said that the bones of
black people were too dense and therefore blacks were
too heavy to be great swimmers.

In 1936, a black man named Matthew Robinson
shattered the Olympic record for the 200 meter dash
and came in second to Jesse Owens. He was in fact
one of the fastest men in known history but was never
mentioned in the same breath as Jesse Owens. He
wound up a janitor in an all-white school while Mr.
Owens was remembered in the same breath as heroes.
Mr. Robinson had a little brother who also had some
degree of athletic ability. His name was the
aforementioned Jackie Robinson.

These are definitely not all of the sports that changed their rules to exclude or control the participation of blacks and other minorities, and, their possible domination of them. There is also Tennis, and Golf, as well as many other sports whose evolution was spurred the addition of minorities.

CHAPTER 13

THE CIVIL RIGHTS ACT

The definition of the word equality
actually means "to be equal". It means to be the same.

13 THE CIVIL RIGHTS ACT

Civil Rights

This chapter is intentionally short because the information can be found in many places. That it even has a place in history is deserving of at least an honorable mention.

The essential Constitution of the United States made provisions to all Americans – in theory. This document endowed each American with certain "unalienable rights" that, under fear of penalty, should not be denied them – in theory. That there would be equal representation and equal opportunity. That there would be equal laws which would allow for equal justice under those equal laws.

But alas, 'twernt to be, as different states or statehood began to interpret these rules more and more liberally which added fuel to the politics of the day. The regional interpretations of these mandated rules and regulations allowed for too much wiggle-room. One state would hold up the rights of some citizens while obliterating the rights of others. The divides fall along the lines of social class, financial status, nationality and oftentimes, skin color. There are of course the afore-mentioned restrictions and or infringements upon the equal distribution of basic human rights.

The conditions that arose from reconstruction after the Civil War were not necessarily in the favor of the ex-slaves. They had to endure hardships and controversy.

They had to overcome the unfair distribution of wealth, possibilities and opportunity. Basic needs were not even being met and punishment for the most insignificant crimes were meted out in massive doses. For example, standing on the sidewalk as whites passed by was punishable by lengthy incarceration. Looking at a white person was sometimes punishable with whipping, and let's not get started with defending oneself against a physical attack – which was often punished with death by lynching.

The worst part about this is, that these actions, or reactions like the devaluation of Black lives were protected under the Federal and State Constitutions. For example, in America, written into the Constitution was the article that said that blacks were to be counted as 3/5 of a person. I guess that then black lives mattered as well, they just didn't matter as much. This was also true when tabulating their votes. Through these actions and legislation arose the need for a government bill that would ensure that the civil rights of one American, would equal the civil rights of all Americans.

Freedom Fighters

Emmett Till:

We are the products of the history our ancestors created, or, were denied.

The unequal treatment of blacks during this era was not more evident than with Emmitt Till. Till was a 14 year old young black man from Chicago who, while visiting relatives in Mississippi in 1955, was accused of whistling at and groped Carolyn Bryant, a white woman. As a result of the accusation, he was murdered, mutilated and discarded. The worst thing about this situation is that Bryant said that she lied. In an interview in early 2017, she admitted that it never happened. Till had done nothing. He was brutalized, beaten, tortured and discarded for NOTHING! To top it off, those who admitted guilt to this crime of murder were acquitted and set free. It was this murder, and subsequent acquittals that sparked the 'Civil Rights Movement'.

Enter the heroism of Rosa Parks and Dr. Martin Luther King Jr. They stood for and preached equality, freedom and civil liberties. Enter Birmingham, Alabama, one of the most racist cities in the world. During these uneasy times, Dr. King organized peaceful marches which were met with violence, prejudice and hatred. The marchers, who were well within their rights, were neither disruptive nor loud but were met with the full brunt of the law. These peaceful marches were met with beatings, water hoses, attack dogs and imprisonment.

Selma, Alabama was also racist, extremely segregated and any movement for voting rights were handled and frowned upon. Even though the marchers' peaceful act was protected under the Constitution of the United States, the governor of Alabama used State Troopers to enforce personal preference. The peaceful, non-violent march was met by Alabama State Troopers with nightsticks, horses and tear gas. It was these specific actions, and many other situations such as these that illuminated the need for a bill to establish equal rights for all. These events are some of the clearest examples of blacks being the reasons for, as well as the beneficiaries of, a Civil Rights Bill.

Even today, there exists the institutional infringement of civil rights in many forms. One such infringement is Loitering Laws which is said to have been a post-Civil War control mechanism. In order to make up for the lack of free labor, many new laws called The Black Codes which included denying freed slaves the right to vote or serve on juries, loitering laws, yearly contracts with former masters – the refusal of which was called vagrancy and was punishable by capital punishment or imprisonment, and, breaking curfew, to name a few. These new laws were directly tied to the Prison Lease Program where inmates were literally rented to companies such as the railroads as laborers for a nominal fee.

Recent incidences of this type of constitutional infringement include a Black man being arrested for waiting in a Starbucks, another Black man arrested for selling individual cigarettes on a street corner and others. In fact, statistics show that Black people are 3 to 10 times more likely to be affected by this selective enforcement of the loitering laws than Whites.. Many of these incidences are so blatant that they are hard to believe. These include the late, great Reverend Martin Luther King being arrested in Montgomery, Alabama for loitering while trying to attend a colleague's court hearing, and, civil rights activist Fred Shuttlesworth being sentenced to 6 months in prison for speaking to friends on a sidewalk during a boycott in Birmingham, Alabama – who was said to have been loitering.

Chicago's 'Gang Loitering Laws' over the course of three years were responsible for about 42,000 arrests of people who merely looked like gang members or had that style of dress. Even the signs in these no loitering zones seemed to have been a little cryptic as below the red "GANG FREE ZONE" words was the word "GANGS" in black letters with a red circle with the line through it only on the "N".

Even though the Supreme Court and many states have found these laws to be unconstitutional, these laws are still impacting primarily Blacks and Latinos today.

Even our current President, businessman Donald Trump has implied that civil rights in their purest forms do not apply equally to all Americans – depending on their genetic make-up. Basically he says that not everyone deserves to have civil rights and he would like to go back to the 'old days' when that sentiment could be openly displayed

CHAPTER 14

ECONOMIC SANCTIONS

It is clearly understood that the foundation of entrepreneurship is capitalism, and capital investment is directly related to the flow of dollars through a community

14 ECONOMIC SANCTIONS

Economic Sanctions

The definition of Economic Sanctions refers to any actions taken by one nation or group of nations to harm the economy of another nation or group – often to force a political or social change. For many policymakers, economic sanctions have become the tool of choice to respond to major geopolitical challenges, from counterterrorism to conflict resolution.

The typical economic sanction is imposed by Governments and multinational bodies to try to alter the strategic decisions of other state and non-state actors that threaten their interests or violate international norms of behavior. The United Nations, the European Union as well as national governments normally impose economic sanctions to impact entities that endanger their interests or violate international policy. Basically, and more frequently, sanctions are the 'slap-on-the-wrists' that precede war. They have been used to advance a range of foreign policy goals, including counterterrorism, genocide, counter-narcotics, nonproliferation, democracy and human rights promotion, cybersecurity and conflict resolution. Sanctions, while a form of intervention, are generally viewed as the lower-cost, lower-risk, middle courses of action between diplomacy and war. Policymakers may consider sanctions a response to foreign crises in which the national interest is less than vital or where military action is not yet feasible. Leaders can on occasion issue sanctions while they evaluate more punitive action. For example, the UN Security Council imposed comprehensive sanctions against Iraq just four days after Saddam Hussein's invasion of Kuwait in August 1990. The Council did not authorize the use of military force until months later.

Critics say sanctions are often poorly conceived and rarely successful in changing a target's conduct, while supporters contend they have become more effective in recent years and remain an essential foreign policy tool. Sanctions are the response of choice to address and counter geopolitical challenges. These sanctions are intended to effect financial relations, as well as, trade, political and security policy. They may be comprehensive, prohibiting commercial activity with regard to an entire country, or they may be tailored for particular businesses, groups, or individuals.
Adapted Sanctions

While it is clear that economic sanctions are normally levied against countries, or other power structures, it is a fact that those same tactics are being, and have been used against blacks, minorities and the poor. The result of which is economic chaos, as it ruins the financial foundation, and even eliminates the possibility of upward mobility.

The sanctions that impact the black and poorer neighborhoods come in many forms including the forms of 'Redlining' and reverse redlining. 'Redlining', is a term coined in the 1960's by sociologist John McKnight referring to the practice of selectively eliminating certain areas from eligibility for loans and/or services based on race or ethnicity. These include banks, insurances, health care and supermarkets, among others who engage in the discriminatory practice of fencing off areas where banks would avoid investments based on community demographics. These are said to have been high-risk areas, unworthy of repayment of loans (even though these areas had a higher rate of repayment than other more affluent areas). I personally remember my first time walking into a bank manager's office and being surprised at seeing a map on the wall with actual red lines drawn around certain neighborhoods. My knowledge of the region let me know that these were the distressed communities that needed this bank's services most.

These dollars often translate into adequate transportation, infrastructure maintenance, housing repair, quality of proper schooling and political representation. Redlining effectively blocks much-needed dollars required by destitute areas from which likely businesses could possibly emerge. It even places these loan-worthy areas at a distinct disadvantage as the residents within them must now rely on outside assistance for even minuscule advancements.

Using the same tactics of unfairly targeting a non-white community, 'Reverse Redlining' floods these same communities with over-priced goods and services – gouging them and luring them into schemes that deplete their bottom line and typically land them into long-term debt. Included in these are loan companies, non-accredited universities and colleges, insurance companies, rent-to-own schemes and any other scheme that offer those looking for hope their 'something-for-nothing'.

Inner city blacks are those most discriminated against using redlining and reverse redlining and their ensuing long-term affects. In the 1980's, in Atlanta for example, results of a Pulitzer Prize-winning series of articles by investigative reporter Bill Dedman revealed that banks would lend to lower-income whites, but not to middle or upper-income blacks. This selective credit rationing is one of the primary reasons blacks are denied access to potential capital for investments, life maintenance or any other improvements.

These opportunities afforded whites allowed them to make advances financially, adding to their bottom lines and boosting their self-esteem, providing the hand-up required by many for these advancements. Redlining contributed heavily to the factors that also helped widen the gap between blacks and whites. Add to this the rhetoric that said civil rights and black freedom contributed to high and rising crime rates and the new slave had a new name – 'criminal'. This is dog-whistle politics at its best. To create more 'criminals' American politicians called for a war on drug users, and drug dealers. Literally hundreds of thousands of people were being jailed for not only selling drugs, but for the misdemeanors of using drugs. John Ehrlichman is quoted as having said:

"...two enemies: the anti-war left and black people. You understand what I'm saying? We knew we couldn't make it illegal to be either against the war or blacks and so by getting the public to associate the hippies with marijuana and blacks with heroin, and then criminalizing both heavily, we could disrupt these communities. We could arrest their leaders, raid their homes, break up their meetings and vilify them night after night on the evening news. Did we know we were lying about the drugs? Of course we did."

Ronald Reagen and his administration begin to dismantle the programs that were set up to assist victims of biased government initiatives that left the poor destitute and struggling. In a speech, Reagen says: *"Yes, there has been an increase in poverty. But, it's a lower rate of increase than with the previous administration – before we got here. It has begun to decline, but it's still going up."*
What???

Gentrification

Almost every city begins the same way - with a focal point. This focal point often comes from the establishment of a school or other small businesses and services. This creates the lure of industry who, are offered tax-incentives to bring manufacturing with products and jobs facilitating upward mobility. For example, a city like Columbus, Ohio was built around the agricultural school The Ohio State University and has developed into the mini-metropolis we see today. These cities then begin to expand outward as support businesses are established and grow, and as a direct result, more employers need and therefore hire more employees. These employees bring with them families, or start families, which require more dwellings.

In the beginning, many of the dwellings are normal, functional housing. As the community begins to prosper, it attracts even more people, whose habitats are normally divided into workforce, management and owners. The dwellings of the workforce were normally built by contractors to be functional and comfortable to accommodate a changing clientele, while management paid for more long-term, single-family housing. The business owners or leaders of these communities typically set themselves apart with more elaborate representations of their wealth.

As it is with upward mobility, the accumulation of wealth reveals itself in the form of upgrades. Included in these upgrades are clothing, transportation, education and dwellings. This creates 'urban sprawl', the expansion of the city's limits. These, the middle-class begins to establish communities and political bases that will favor their interests and children, setting themselves apart from the 'lower-classes'.

The cycle of gentrification normally begins with what is termed ,white-flight'. This phenomenon involves the migration of white families to suburban areas when minorities and the poor move into the neighborhoods wherein they currently reside. This can be directly attributed to assimilation and association and the result thereof. Many of those of European descent have been taught by their elders the perils of diluting heritage and wealth. They are taught that the poor almost always squander wealth due to genetic inferiority and ignorance, and, create weaker offspring, incapable of proper function. These fears, which are founded on eugenics, when one looks at ‚Black Wall Street‘ and other affluent minority communities, have been proven to be unfounded and not necessarily true. So, to insure separation of ‚races‘ and classes, these aforementioned lower-classes are villainized and downgraded as subhuman and shunned by the affluent. This insures that the wealth, bloodlines and perceived superior genes stay somewhat pure and that the wealth remains in a smaller circle.

What normally happens when the middle-class and affluent move out, the poor and lower-classes move in. And as many of these dwellings are not very well maintained, and the repairs must be done within a certain budget, they begin to take on other characteristics – namely deterioration.

What gentrification does is create a standard, typically through 'Historical Designation', which requires that the buildings and dwellings are restored to the original standard with original pieces and parts. The issue with this is that when a neighborhood is deemed historic, all the pieces of the dwellings with this designation must be original or fabricated exactly to the original specs. The fact is, all those parts cost far more than they're worth and many of those who took those properties over from the original owners cannot afford to bring them up to the newly established code. The result of this situation is the displacement of the poor as the 'Government' mandates compliance for any place deemed historic.

The phenomenon of white flight seemed to have been due to both racism and economic reasons, though the jury is still out on that one. After the Second World War, about 4 million blacks migrated from the rural south to the northern regions of the USA. As these blacks settled in the industrial areas in the north and west circa 1940 thru 1970, this apparently spurred white movement to the suburbs. Many, including Ta-Nehisi Coates believe that this migration was directly due the influx of blacks into these communities. It is clear that many families sought larger housing and safer neighborhoods due to their prosperity after the war. It is equally clear that these new prospective Black neighbors were systematically prevented from entering these neighborhoods by real estate agents and mortgage brokers. One well-known example of this was then businessman Donald Trump and his father being prosecuted for racial discrimination in housing. It is documented that Trump Management refused to allow minorities into their properties, even though many of the prospects held high degrees and were more than financially qualified.

So the question raised by this paradigm is why did they leave? Was it for racial or economic reasons? One fact is clear - when black people moved in, white people moved out. Yet only a portion of white flight can be traced back to the now-classic dynamic of racial turnover. Previously, cities were simply too segregated by race for many urban whites to encounter black neighbors. Newly available Census Bureau maps show that in 1940, the average white urban household lived three miles away from a black enclave. By 1970, urban areas adjacent to historical black enclaves became predominantly black, but distant city neighborhoods remained predominantly white — no different in racial composition from the surrounding suburbs.

Another of the main reasons for white-flight was, and remains, the tax rate. Because voters from suburban areas paid higher taxes they received higher-quality services including maintenance, roads, schools, and police protection while minorities and the poor in these gentrified neighborhoods wound up evicted or otherwise displaced due to the rising prices.

The voters from the cities were poor and more racially diverse than the more affluent who desired low property taxes as well as higher-quality public services. In fact, for this set of households, what mattered most about the new Southern arrivals crowding into neighborhoods across town was not their race but their lower levels of income.

That doesn't mean racism wasn't a motivating factor. For the third of white households near a black enclave in 1940, concerns about new black neighbors was indeed a primary motivation. As a result, those households moved out of the city at a higher rate than others, contributing more than a third to the white exodus. But for the remainder of urban whites, most of whom never interacted with a black family, leaving for the resource-rich suburbs was an economic calculus, one that was accelerated by the steady stream of poor migrants, both white and black, into central cities.

Just like Trump voters in 2016, different people in the same group — white urban households — took the same action, around the same time, but for different reasons. To complicate the picture, few of them left personal accounts, and they may not have been able to articulate exactly why they moved. We are left reconstructing the pieces through careful detective work. In my own work, I have found that Poirot is often right: Each suspect wielded his own knife.

A 2010 study on "Who Gentrifies Low-Income Neighborhoods" found that the impact of gentrification on black residents varies based on level of education. By examining around 15,000 census tracts in 64 metros from 1990 to 2000, the authors found that gentrification tends to benefit highly educated black households. In fact, one-third of the increase in income among gentrifying neighborhoods during this period came from the progress of this specific demographic. This in turn causes gentrifying neighborhoods to be more attractive to middle-class black households. But gentrification can also have a negative effect on less educated black households, by pushing those who did not complete high school out of gentrifying neighborhoods.

That said, displacement can be and is a big issue in places where gentrification is occurring at a feverish pace. In her coverage of related research by the UC Berkeley Urban Displacement Project, Tanvi Misra points to the strong link between gentrification and displacement in a high-gentrification city like San Francisco. Over a quarter of San Francisco's neighborhoods (422 of the nearly 1,600 surveyed) are at risk of displacement. The study's lead author, Karen Chapple, writes that by 2030, San Francisco, Oakland, "and many other Bay Area communities may realize that their neighborhood has turned the corner from displacement risk to reality."

Indeed, displacement is becoming a larger issue in knowledge hubs and superstar cities, where the pressure for urban living is accelerating. These particular cities attract new businesses, highly skilled workers, major developers, and large corporations, all of which drive up both the demand for and cost of housing. As a result, local residents, and neighborhood renters in particular, may feel pressured to move to more affordable locations.

The reality is that the displaced are getting pushed out of working-class neighborhoods that are "good enough" to attract people and investment, while the poorest and most vulnerable neighborhoods remain mired in persistent poverty and concentrated disadvantage.

All of which points to the biggest, most crucial task ahead: creating more inclusive cities and neighborhoods that can meet the needs of all urbanites, as well as adjoining suburbanites.

The 'War' on Drugs

While the War on Drugs actually began with a declining rate of illegal drug use, it resulted in a rate of incarceration higher than anywhere else in the world. This rate is disproportionate in terms of race; while people of all colors use and sell at the same rate, blacks are imprisoned at rates twenty to fifty times higher than those for whites. There is also not much of a correlation between crime and punishment; sociologists point out that governments decide what they want to punish regardless of crime rates.

Drug Addiction

Drug addiction, specifically Opium, Cocaine and heroin, has been a serious issue for Americans since the 19th century. They were used, along with alcohol for pain and to treat many other ailments. The opium addiction came about as a result of the Civil War when wounded soldiers were treated with it on battlefields to ease their pain. This ushered in its non-medical use as those who left the military were already addicted.

In the late 1900's, the Asian influence with their opium dens (not unlike the crack houses of today) saw a substantial rise in addiction among Chinese immigrants and the Caucasian underground with its prostitutes, gamblers and other criminals. The ensuing victims were upper and middle class white women who were prescribed opium, morphine and laudamum for menstrual and menopausal discomfort. This iatrogenic addiction was the result of continued treatment where the afflicted built up tolerances, thereby needing to increase dosage. The late 19th into the early 20th saw those women and war veterans afflicted being treated with sympathy and understanding. Then, the focus was on curing them and reinserting them into society. However, many of those released from treatment centers and sanitariums suffered relapses.

The Pure Food and Drug Act of 1906 mandated that all medicines containing opioids write it on their labels. In 1914, The Harrison Narcotic Act, at the possible risk of big pharma, the federal government imposed restrictions on opioids in medicines. This Act basically legalized the presence of opioids in medicine through regulation.

The ongoing debate about drug addiction centers around two points: Either addiction is an incurable disease that requires long-term handling with medication; or, Addiction's roots lie in weak morals, broken will and environmental influence best handled by criminalizing usage and distribution.

This debate is the focus of this chapter. Why was, and is white America treated differently in the matters of drug use and addiction?

The crop of addicted were immigrants who were in the U.S. without employment or opportunities. The drugs offered an inexpensive release from their stress and pain. They younger women also rebelled with Jazz, alcohol, their choices of clothing and yes, drugs as they tired of being downtrodden and treated as second-class citizens.

Over time, one can see the changes in the political, social, legal and medical treatment responses based on race and socioeconomic hierarchy and/or affiliation.
The 1930's and 1940's saw a shift from empathetic drug addiction treatment to the criminalization of any illegal drug association. After WWII, the migration of Europeans and Asians from the ghettos, coupled with the influx of Hispanics and African Americans shifted the focus of government and law enforcement in their direction. The fear of this new demographic created new targets. All that was left to do was to villainize them.

The Vietnam Nam War was responsible for a new influx of heroin addicts as many soldiers were addicted or at least tried the drug. By the mid 1980's, there were at least 500,000 people addicted to opioids in the U.S. becoming a social as well as medical concern. So, even though there were alternatives to mass incarceration of specifically drug users, the administration of this time chose to give the majority of these Hispanics and African Americans maximum sentences.

The public and administration responded with new legislation - 'The War on Drugs' which focused on the criminalization of distributing or even using illegal substances.
The findings of certain studies revealed that drug treatment was much more cost effective than the penalties levied against these users. A study on the

effectiveness, cost and benefits of drug abuse treatment was done by the California Department of Alcohol and Drug Programs. A thorough investigation using provider records, databases and follow up interviews with treatment participants shed new light on drug-related activity. This included of course drug and alcohol usage, criminal activity and involvement, health and health care and even income. The study also focused on the costs of treatment and the economic value of these treatments to society. The California Drug and Alcohol Treatment Assessment found that:

- Treatment was cost beneficial to taxpayers, with the cost averaging $7 returned for every dollar invested "Each day of treatment paid for itself (the benefits to taxpaying citizens *equaled* or exceeded treatment costs) on the day it was received, primarily through an avoidance of crime". "Regardless of the modality of care, treatment-related economic savings outweighed costs by at least 4 to 1".

- Methadone treatment was among the most cost-effective treatments, yielding savings of $3 to $4 for every dollar spent. This was true for each major methadone treatment modality, but costs were lower in an outpatient OTP than in a residential or social modality.

- Patients in methadone maintenance showed the greatest reduction in intensity of heroin use, down by two-thirds, of any type of opioid addiction treatment studied.

- Patients in methadone maintenance showed the greatest reductions in criminal activity and drug selling, down 84 percent and 86 percent, respectively, of any type of opioid addiction treatment studied.

- Health care use decreased for all treatment modalities; participants in methadone maintenance treatment showed the greatest reduction in the number of days of hospitalization, down 57.6 percent, of any modality.

So, having this knowledge and the data that supports treatment over incarceration, why did the onslaught on the black community even take place? Add to that the Narcotic Addict Treatment Act of 1974, and the availability of methadone treatment outlined in the National Institutes of Health findings in 1977, why enact the three strikes law targeting these drug addicted residents?

In the eighties mandatory minimums for the mere usage of drugs were stressed. Now that the opium has hit Appalachia, the government wants to do away with those minimums and rehabilitation is now preferred.

Three strikes...

Why were these addicts attacked with the full brunt of the law and those who are currently suffering in Appalachia receiving sympathetic support from the same government? The black thread continues...

Gun Control Laws

The Second Amendment to the Constitution of the United States, as well as the Bill of Rights provide for the right to keep and bear arms. This was true and enforced until Blacks of the 60's and 70's, having been brutalized and beaten (especially Los Angeles and New York), decided, in their own defense, to exercise that right. The second amendment states:

"A well-regulated Militia, being necessary to the security of a free state, the right of the people to keep and bear Arms, shall not be infringed."

I understand the need for some gun control regulations due to a number of shootings with automatic weapons resulting in the deaths of innocents. It seems that there were those with psychological disorders who were allowed to purchase these weapons and used then against fellow citizens. The fact that this happened all over the world only added fuel to this already smoldering issue.

Some want true gun control including longer waiting periods and criminal and psychological background checks. Others want to take weapons out of the hands of citizens all together. The problem with the latter is that when only the authorities possess weapons, that allows them ultimate control, and that is a slippery slope indeed.

The Black Panthers Change History

The 'Black Panthers for Self-Defense' was a national benevolent, self-help organization created in 1966 by Huey Newton and Bobby Sealle to offset the system of white oppression. The Panther's central guiding principle was "Undying love for the people" the focus of which was to protect, feed and educate the blacks that lived in these distressed areas. They established food-banks, schools, hospitals and drug rehabilitation centers, and became responsible for the welfare of the inhabitants of these communities. For example, two hours every morning, they provided their 'Breakfast for Children' program feeding impoverished children and youth.

In 1966, just like today, police brutality took a turn for the worse. As a result of these brutal attacks, the Panthers launched a series of protests, which included the armed surveillance of police arrests in black communities, as it was then lawful to openly carry a weapon.

In 1967, the Panthers launched a peaceful protest in the form of walking into the courthouse with loaded rifles (which was a lawful act), to address racial issues that existed in California at the time. The then Director of the FBI J. Edgar Hoover called these radicals a 'black nationalist, hate-type organization' and deemed them 'public enemy number 1'. This fear of the rise of the Black Panther Party prompted Hoover to create the clandestine operation, 'COINTELPRO'. The job of this counterintelligence organization was to discredit Black Nationalist groups through exposing, misdirecting or disrupting their activities. In fact, in 1967, an FBI informant helped train and provide arms to the Panthers.

As a result of the success of the Panthers and their appeal to the youth and other blacks in the nation, the State of California enlisted the help of the NRA to invoke the Mulford Act under then Governor Ronald Reagan. The purpose of this act was to restrict citizens from carrying guns in public and created strict gun control legislation. That sentiment was echoed throughout the entire country until the NRA lobbied for hard-line advocation of gun ownership rights in the late 1970's and early 80's when Reagan changed his stance as well.

Today, as social media allows more access to current events as they occur, we see that there is still a disparity in the way whites and people of color are treated when it comes to gun laws.

D. W. Griffeth's 'Birth of a Nation' was responsible for the resurgence of the Ku Klux Klan. Its purpose was to erase the South's loss of the Civil War. The KKK was romanticized as heroes and saviors of the white race against the black 'animals'. This sparked terrorism in the forms of murder, and beatings and lynching against blacks who, then fled from the south to L.A., New York, Chicago, Cleveland, Detroit and Boston. These include the aforementioned Emmett Till, who was beaten to death beyond recognition in Mississippi in 1955 for allegedly whistling at and groping Carolyn Bryant, (a white woman), peaceful marches to address the absence of civil rights, accusing and convicting black men of crimes when they were proven to have been somewhere else and other inequalities in the justice system, and, as we also mentioned before, the multiple bombings of churches. When public outcry began to frown upon the outward murder and torture of blacks, the powers that be came up with different strategies which included 'segregation', 'Jim Crow', voting restrictions and the like. Like today, the economic reform and tax laws insured that there would always be a divide between blacks and whites. Tools such as the voting questionnaires from Louisiana, loitering laws and three strikes laws targeting drug users, (of which we previously spoke), insure that gap only gets wider.

<u>The 13th Amendment</u>

The Thirteenth Amendment (Amendment XIII) to the United States Constitution abolished slavery and involuntary servitude, except as punishment for a crime. An important nuance of this development is in the wording. Dr. Ulmer Johnson during an interview on the widely acclaimed radio show, 'The Breakfast Club', hosted by DJ Envy, Angela Yee, and Charlamagne tha God, explained that *emancipation* only makes you free inside a certain system. He also explains the difference between 'freedom' and 'liberty' –
freedom having to do with *all-access and privilege;* while *liberty* is *permission to move within a system*.

A shocking statistic is that America makes up 5% of the world's population, but accounts for 25% of its prison systems. This 'cash-crop' is a tree with many branches and roots that dig down into mother earth herself.

Tougher Laws

3 Strikes Law & Privatization of our Prison System

Welcome the privatization of the prison system and the 'Convict Lease Program 2.0', which is today's version of the original.

The privatization of America's prison system took root in the early 1980's. The 'Corrections Corporation of America' founded in 1983 by Thomas Beasley, Doctor R. Crants, and T. Don Hutto, introduced the idea of running prisons for profit. In an issue of 'Inc. Magazine', one the founders stated: *"You just sell it like you were selling cars, or real estate, or hamburgers..."*.

Today, corporate-run prisons hold eight percent of America's inmates. Here's how the private prison industry began. After running a county jail and a juvenile detention center in Tennessee in 1984, it CCA opened its first privately owned facility in Houston (a former hotel adapted to house immigration detainees). A year later, CCA tries unsuccessfully to secure a 99 year lease on Tennessee's entire prison system for $250 million. In 1986, CCA goes public with claims that its facility would need less staff than public prisons due to its use of electronic surveillance.

Mirroring the Ray Crock model, and for tax purposes, CCA becomes a real estate investment trust, which allowed them to claim they were in the property business. Their new affiliate, Prison Realty Trust's $447 million prison buying spree elevated the demand for inmates to fill them. Since the private prison system was about money and little else, minimum-security facilities were filled with maximum-security inmates, guarded by inexperienced guards. This prompted a 1998 Justice Department probe in Youngstown, Ohio which, found this to be the case.

It seems that the formula for implementation of these types of facilities includes starting with running an immigration detention center like the GEO Group, originally known as the Wackenhut Corrections Corporation.

It was really the 'Three-Strikes Legislation' and ''Truth-in-Sentencing' laws co-chaired by CCA and the American Legislative Exchange Council that marked the turning point in 90's prison population numbers. The plummeting CCA stock share price prompted the private prison system to take drastic measures.

- **2000**

As prison occupancy rates drop, Prison Realty Trust nearly goes bankrupt. CCA stock, once nearly $150 a share, falls to 19 cents. The company drops the trust and restructures.

- **2004**

A Justice Department report finds a "disturbing degree" of physical abuse by staff and underreporting of violence among inmates at a Baltimore juvenile facility run by the private prison operator Correctional Services Corporation. CSC is later acquired by GEO.

- **2005**

Rep. Ted Strickland (D-Ohio) introduces the Private Prison Information Act, which would require private prisons holding federal inmates to comply with Freedom of Information Act requests. It died, as have at least seven similar bills opposed by CCA and GEO.

- **2007**

CCA's and GEO's stock prices jump as both companies jockey to run the federal government's expanding immigration detention centers. Meanwhile, the ACLU settles a case against Immigration and Customs Enforcement for conditions in the CCA-managed T. Don Hutto Residential Center in Texas, where about half the detainees are kids. Under the agreement, children no longer wear prison uniforms and may move more freely.

- **2008**

The New York Times investigates the deaths of immigration detainees, such as a Guinean man at a CCA-run facility who fractured his skull and was placed in solitary confinement before being taken to a hospital. He died after four months in a coma.

- **2009**

A CCA representative attends a meeting where ALEC members draft the legislation that will eventually become Arizona's notorious anti-immigration law. CCA denies having a hand in writing the bill. It cuts ties with ALEC the following year.

- **2010**

An ACLU suit alleges rampant violence at a CCA-run Idaho prison known as "gladiator school." The lawsuit claims the prison is understaffed and fosters an environment that "relies on the degradation, humiliation, and subjugation of prisoners." The FBI investigates but doesn't pursue charges. In Kentucky, the governor orders all female inmates removed from a CCA prison after more than a dozen cases of alleged sexual abuse by guards.

- **2011**

CCA becomes the first private prison company to purchase a state facility, buying Ohio's Lake Erie Correctional Institution as part of a privatization plan proposed by Gov. John Kasich and supported by his corrections chief, former CCA Director Gary Mohr.

- **2012**

CCA offers to buy prisons in 48 states in exchange for 20-year management contracts. The same year, a GEO-operated youth facility in Mississippi where staff sexually abused minors is described by a judge as a "cesspool of unconstitutional and inhuman acts and conditions." At another Mississippi facility, a 24-year-old CCA employee is killed during a riot over prisoners' complaints about poor food, inadequate medical care, and disrespectful guards.

- **2013**

CCA converts back to a real estate investment trust, as does GEO. Mother Jones reports that the Bill & Melinda Gates Foundation has invested $2.2 million in GEO.

- **2014**

As it did during at least the previous five years, CCA's annual report flags criminal justice reform - including drug decriminalization and the reduction of mandatory minimum sentences—as a "risk factor" for its business.*_ Chris Epps, Mississippi's prison commissioner and the president of the American Correctional Association, is charged with taking kickbacks from a private prison contractor.

• **2015**

Sen. Bernie Sanders (I-Vt.) co-sponsors the Justice is Not for Sale Act, which would ban all government contracts with private prison companies. After Hillary Clinton is criticized for using campaign bundlers who'd worked as lobbyists for CCA and GEO, she promises to no longer take their money and says, "We should end private prisons and private detention centers."

Activists believe the low-cost prison labor force is why many laws have been changed from misdemeanors to felonies – to fill up the prisons. It is the reason Nixon turned the possession of marijuana from a misdemeanor to a first class felony and the Clintons enacted the three strikes law.

You see, each prisoner is worth about $40,000 per year. Make the minimum sentence 10 years, and these incarcerated 'slaves' suddenly become worth $400,000 each. Multiply that figure by 1000-3000 prisoners in each prison and a new investment opportunity presents itself. (2000 x 40,000 = 80,000,000 dollars per year - guaranteed). That's what the tax-payers pay to keep 'criminals' incarcerated. Add to this the products they produce and the services they are forced to provide, and you have a recipe for printing money. The annual revenue stream from the private prison systems topple $100 Billion in America alone.

At the end of the Ronald Reagan administration, 225 of the cabinet members quit, were fired, arrested, convicted or indicted on criminal charges or violating the ethics code. Even America's highest-ranking law enforcement official, Attorney General Edwin Mees was investigated by no less than three special prosecutors. To understand why this is important or why it's relevant one needs to know that the Reagan platform ran on cracking down on street-criminals and were elected by the 'moral majority'. The criminals to which they referred were low-income or poorer individuals in distressed communities. So, in effect, the government pushing for the incarceration of 'street-criminals' were themselves committing high crime.

During this time, inner city drug addicts were seen as criminals and given mandatory minimum sentences in prison. Even today, in the South, there is a phenomenon called the 'Opioid Addiction' that plagues poor and middle class whites. This is said to need understanding and sympathy.

Disproportionate policing of whites and blacks is evidenced by the examples of a white man in Florida stabbing and killing two people, stabbing another and then eating his face - being only tazed by authorities before apprehension; In Colorado, a white man kills twelve and he's taken alive; and, in Charleston, the murderer of nine parishioners was taken alive and because he said he was hungry, taken to Burger King before being taken in.

On the other hand, two black men, one selling CD's and the other loose cigarettes were shot and killed. Were blacks the reason we now have low or no-tolerance laws? The evidence points to yes.

I have listed the names of some of those blacks shot by police (most of which are questionable), in this, the new millennium:

- David McAtee, August 3, 1966 - June 1, 2020
- George Perry Floyd, October 14, 1973 - May 25, 2020
- Dreasjon "Sean" Reed, 1999 - May 6, 2020
- Michael Brent Charles Ramos, January 1, 1978 - April 24, 2020
- Breonna Taylor, June 5, 1993 - March 13, 2020
- Manuel "Mannie" Elijah Ellis, August 28, 1986 - March 3, 2020
- Atatiana Koquice Jefferson, November 28, 1990 - October 12, 2019
- Emantic "EJ" Fitzgerald Bradford Jr., June 18, 1997 - November 22, 2018
- Charles "Chop" Roundtree Jr., September 5, 2000 - October 17, 2018
- Chinedu Okobi, February 13, 1982 - October 3, 2018
- Botham Shem Jean, September 29, 1991 - September 6, 2018

- Antwon Rose Jr., July 12, 2000 - June 19, 2018
- Saheed Vassell, December 22, 1983 - April 4, 2018
- Stephon Alonzo Clark, August 10, 1995 - March 18, 2018
- Aaron Bailey, 1972 - June 29, 2017
- Charleena Chavon Lyles, April 24, 1987 - June 18, 2017
- Fetus of Charleena Chavon Lyles (14-15 weeks), June 18, 2017
- Jordan Edwards, October 25, 2001 - April 29, 2017

- Chad Robertson, 1992 - February 15, 2017
- Deborah Danner, September 25, 1950 - October 18, 2016
- Alfred Olango, July 29, 1978 - September 27, 2016
- Terence Crutcher, August 16, 1976 - September 16, 2016
- Terrence LeDell Sterling, July 31, 1985 - September 11, 2016
- Korryn Gaines, August 24, 1993 - August 1, 2016
- Joseph Curtis Mann, 1966 - July 11, 2016
- Philando Castile, July 16, 1983 - July 6, 2016
- Alton Sterling, June 14, 1979 - July 5, 2016
- Bettie "Betty Boo" Jones, 1960 - December 26, 2015
- Quintonio LeGrier, April 29, 1996 - December 26, 2015
- Corey Lamar Jones, February 3, 1984 - October 18, 2015
- Jamar O'Neal Clark, May 3, 1991 - November 16, 2015
- Jeremy "Bam Bam" McDole, 1987 - September 23, 2015
- India Kager, June 9, 1988 - September 5, 2015

- Samuel Vincent DuBose, March 12, 1972 - July 19, 2015
- Sandra Bland, February 7, 1987 - July 13, 2015
- Brendon K. Glenn, 1986 - May 5, 2015
- Freddie Carlos Gray Jr., August 16, 1989 - April 19, 2015
- Walter Lamar Scott, February 9, 1965 - April 4, 2015
- Eric Courtney Harris, October 10, 1971 - April 2, 2015
- Phillip Gregory White, 1982 - March 31, 2015
- Mya Shawatza Hall, December 5, 1987 - March 30, 2015
- Meagan Hockaday, August 27, 1988 - March 28, 2015
- Tony Terrell Robinson, Jr., October 18, 1995 - March 6, 2015
- Janisha Fonville, March 3, 1994 - February 18 2015
- Natasha McKenna, January 9, 1978 - February 8, 2015
- Jerame C. Reid, June 8, 1978 - December 30, 2014
- Rumain Brisbon, November 24, 1980 - December 2, 2014
- Tamir Rice, June 15, 2002 - November 22, 2014
- Akai Kareem Gurley, November 12, 1986 - November 20, 2014
- Tanisha N. Anderson, January 22, 1977 - November 13, 2014
- Dante Parker, August 14, 1977 - August 12, 2014
- Ezell Ford, October 14, 1988 - August 11, 2014
- Michael Brown Jr., May 20, 1996 - August 9, 2014
- John Crawford III, July 29, 1992 - August 5, 2014
- Eric Garner, September 15, 1970 - July 17, 2014
- Dontre Hamilton, January 20, 1983 - April 30, 2014

- Victor White III, September 11, 1991 - March 3, 2014
- Gabriella Monique Nevarez, November 25, 1991 - March 2, 2014
- Yvette Smith, December 18, 1966 - February 16, 2014
- McKenzie J. Cochran, August 25, 1988 - January 29, 2014
- Jordan Baker, 1988 - January 16, 2014
- Andy Lopez, June 2, 2000 - October 22, 2013
  Miriam Iris Carey, August 12, 1979 - October 3, 2013
- Barrington "BJ" Williams, 1988 - September 17, 2013
- Jonathan Ferrell, October 11, 1989 - September 14, 2013
- Carlos Alcis, 1970 - August 15, 2013
- Larry Eugene Jackson Jr., November 29, 1980 - July 26, 2013
- Kyam Livingston, July 29, 1975 - July 21, 2013
- Clinton R. Allen, September 26, 1987 - March 10, 2013
- Kimani "KiKi" Gray, October 19, 1996 - March 9, 2013
- Kayla Moore, April 17, 1971 - February 13, 2013
- Jamaal Moore Sr., 1989 - December 15, 2012
- Johnnie Kamahi Warren, February 26, 1968 - February 13, 2012
- Shelly Marie Frey, April 21, 1985 - December 6, 2012
- Darnisha Diana Harris, December 11, 1996 - December 2, 2012
- Timothy Russell, December 9. 1968 - November 29, 2012

- Malissa Williams, June 20, 1982 - November 29, 2012
- Noel Palanco, November 28, 1989 - October 4, 2012
- Reynaldo Cuevas, January 6, 1992 - September 7, 2012
- Chavis Carter, 1991 - July 28, 2012
- Alesia Thomas, June 1, 1977 - July 22, 2012
- Shantel Davis, May 26, 1989 - June 14, 2012
- Sharmel T. Edwards, October 10, 1962 - April 21, 2012
- Tamon Robinson, December 21, 1985 - April 18, 2012
- Ervin Lee Jefferson, III, 1994 - March 24, 2012
- Kendrec McDade, May 5, 1992 - March 24, 2012
- Rekia Boyd, November 5, 1989 - March 21, 2012
- Shereese Francis, 1982 - March 15, 2012
- Jersey K. Green, June 17, 1974 - March 12, 2012
- Wendell James Allen, December 19, 1991 - March 7, 2012
- Nehemiah Lazar Dillard, July 29, 1982 - March 5, 2012
- Dante' Lamar Price, July 18, 1986 - March 1, 2012
- Raymond Luther Allen Jr., 1978 - February 29, 2012
- Manual Levi Loggins Jr., February 22, 1980 - February 7, 2012
- Ramarley Graham, April 12, 1993 - February 2, 2012
- Kenneth Chamberlain Sr., April 12, 1943 - November 19, 2011
- Alonzo Ashley, June 10, 1982 - July 18, 2011
- Derek Williams, January 23, 1989 - July 6, 2011
- Raheim Brown, Jr., March 4, 1990 - January 22, 2011

- Reginald Doucet, June 3, 1985 - January 14, 2011
- Derrick Jones, September 30, 1973 - November 8, 2010
- Danroy "DJ" Henry Jr., October 29, 1990 - October 17, 2010
- Aiyana Mo'Nay Stanley-Jones, July 20, 2002 - May 16, 2010
- Steven Eugene Washington, September 20, 1982 - March 20, 2010
- Aaron Campbell, September 7, 1984 - January 29, 2010
- Kiwane Carrington, July 14, 1994 - October 9, 2009
- Victor Steen, November 11, 1991 - October 3, 2009
- Shem Walker, March 18, 1960 - July 11, 2009
- Oscar Grant III, February 27, 1986 - January 1, 2009
- Tarika Wilson, October 30, 1981 - January 4, 2008
- DeAunta Terrel Farrow, September 7, 1994 - June 22, 2007
- Sean Bell, May 23, 1983 - November 25, 2006
- Kathryn Johnston, June 26, 1914 - November 21, 2006
- Ronald Curtis Madison, March 1, 1965 - September 4, 2005
- James B. Brissette Jr., November 6, 1987 - September 4, 2005
- Henry "Ace" Glover, October 2, 1973 - September 2, 2005
- Timothy Stansbury, Jr., November 16, 1984 - January 24, 2004
- Ousmane Zongo, 1960 - May 22, 2003
- Alberta Spruill, 1946 - May 16, 2003
- Kendra Sarie James, December 24, 1981 - May 5, 2003
- Orlando Barlow, December 29, 1974 - February 28, 2003

- Timothy DeWayne Thomas Jr., July 25, 1981 - April 7, 2001
- Ronald Beasley, 1964 - June 12, 2000
- Earl Murray, 1964 - June 12, 2000
- Patrick Moses Dorismond, February 28, 1974 - March 16, 2000
- Prince Carmen Jones Jr., March 30, 1975 - September 1, 2000
- Malcolm Ferguson, October 31, 1976 - March 1, 2000
- LaTanya Haggerty, 1973 - June 4, 1999

We must add to this list *Trayvon Martin* and *James Davis Jr.* (they were murdered by citizens who were not charged).

There seems to be a pattern here. I'm not condemning ALL police or non-blacks – but this fiber of the thread deserves special attention.

A BLACK THREAD

CHAPTER 15

MUSIC

"If one should desire to know whether a kingdom is well governed, if its morals are good or bad, the quality of music will furnish the answer."
Confucius.

15 MUSIC

A Natural Phenomenon

Music is an ancient phenomenon stemming from human, and other natural sounds and rhythms. The combinations of these sounds as tones, patterns and repetition were used as entertainment and also had practical, as well as religious functions. The application of these energies, frequencies and vibrations have, and will forever change our very existence.

"If one should desire to know whether a kingdom is well governed, if its morals are good or bad, the quality of music will furnish the answer." Confucius.

Since the beginning of time, people have used music to tell stories and convey feelings with and without instruments. Music is the pulse through which history is told. Just play a style of music or melody and you are transported instantly to that era or culture. Music is also the ultimate personification of creativity. Almost anyone can create a beat or hum a melody, or at least think them.

One thing that bothers me personally is that the creativity that is the foundation of a brilliant, high-end representation of American ingenuity is typically associated with poverty, degradation and subjugation. I understand that the spiritual genre IN AMERICA began with slaves. The point of the matter is that the true source of the spiritual genre came WITH the slaves. These slaves, who were in many cases doctors, musicians, royalty, scientists, mathematicians, authors, astronomers and more - these great movers and shakers were already accomplished in their prospective fields and being mixed in together allowed them to bond through the melodies and rhythms. I believe that the main reason there was humming while working is that there were songs written in different languages, as the divide and conquer application made sure that those of different languages were grouped together.

In African and Eastern culture, music was used as the fifth element. It was used to inspire, uplift, excite and heal. So, when the slaves were singing and or humming, they were healing themselves and each other. Having had an understanding of quantum physics, they were instinctively using sound to rearrange the molecules within themselves, and all around them. So to say that African American music began with slavery is a disrespectful atrocity that robs an entire culture of a tremendous contribution and erroneously attributes said contribution to a situation created by selfishness and greed.

We could go all the way back beyond Mesopotamia, even before the Zingh empire, but for our purposes, we'll begin with Egypt.

History of Instruments

Whether the Egyptians or their Jewish slaves were responsible for maintaining and advancing modern music remains a topic of discussion. DNA evidence proves that many of the Haitians, Jamaicans, Hispanics, Amerindians, Hawaiians and many more can be traced back to ancient Egypt. This means that these two cultures, both being brown are clear sources of styles of music and musical instruments including:

- the Ney - predecessor to the flute;
- the Qanun - a stringed instrument not unlike the guitar;.
- the Arghul – very similar to the Saxofon;
- the Mizmar – a double-reeded instrument like the Woodwinds of today;
- the Sistrum, drum, tambourine and castanets - all percussion instruments; and of course, Trumpets.

These instruments influenced the development of the structure of modern music and music throughout time from the Persians and Greeks to the Romans, from the Arabs to the Europeans.

Influencing Culture

So, how are Black people responsible for influencing the international musical culture? All music does two things simultaneously: It reflects the culture whence it comes, and, influences every culture that accepts, or even rejects it. A blaring example is America, whose founders' roots lay in Europe and therefore whose music reflects that culture. But, the strength of American music, or, its identity is clearly a product of the African-American sub-culture as represented by the style, dress and languages born of it.

It's not just the rhythms and beats (although they comprise a major part), it is also the text, tempo, form and flow. Today's music is greatly influenced by syncopated rhythms and the pentatonic scale (ironically, the black keys), which originated in West Africa.

The Pentatonic Scale and Reconstruction

The most famous, most recorded spiritual of all time, Amazing Grace' is credited to have been written by English poet and Anglican Clergymen John Newton. He was also involved with the Atlantic Slave Trade and wrote the song while in a storm aboard ship. How ironic that the credits to Amazing Grace says „words by John Newton - music by unknown". When one understands that this melody was written using the pentatonic scale, and that the pentatonic scale comes from West Africa, this ‚unknown' becomes quite clear. Historians believe that Newton heard the slaves in the galley below deck singing their unknown song of lamentation as a result of the tumultuous seas upon which they sailed being tossed to and fro, not knowing their fate. This melody, containing only the five notes of the West African scale became the standard for most of the ‚Negro Spirituals' in existence.

During the Civil War and beyond, ex-slaves and other African Americans became part of military bands, learning diatonic harmony and combining it with the natural harmonic series and blue notes (or, the Dorian scale), birthing the blues and ragtime. The soul of the blues was felt in everything from jazz to rock, country music to rhythm and blues, and classical music. To hear the blues' influence on classical music, I recommend 'Rhapsody in Blue' by George Gershwin.

Gospel

The genre ,Gospel' was created and popularized by Thomas A. Dorsey, or ,Georgia Tom' as he was known around Blues circles. The Blues was a continuation of Negro Spirituals sang and performed in bars, clubs and speakeasies, usually associated with alcohol, relationships and other general problems associated with Reconstruction. This style, through improvisation evolved into the mixture of ragtime and blues, or Jazz. From Jazz came Big Band.

The pre-cursor of gospel music was Ragtime, a style of stride piano introduced by composer Scott Joplin, also made popular by his protégés Arthur Marshall, Scott Hayden and Brun Campbell. Ragtime spawned the secular spiritual music known as the ,Blues' as many musicians who could not afford formal training learned to play without notes or ,by ear' as it is known even today. The ongoing debate, however unnecessary, is what yields the better musician, as both can be competent, professional additions to ensembles. Those fortunate enough (or, unfortunate, depending on how you look at it), to have formal training, open themselves up to knowledge of the ages but are limited by the rules of those institutions. Those who play from their soul, or by ear, draw upon the information in their prospective environments. It becomes the difference between becoming a part of a culture, or, creating one.

Whether or not heredity or DNA plays a role or is a factor at all is a question for those much smarter than me, however, my grandparents, mother and father were all musically inclined, and the first time I sat on a set of drums, I could play them. I also, without formal training, I am able to play at least 12 instruments on an accomplished level and sing at least 4 ½ octaves.

Jazz – The Freedom of Improvisation

The improvisation of these melodies became jazz. The creativity of infusing syncopated polyrhythms into this music spawned new dances based on the beats in between 1, 2, 3 and 4. The music freed the energy processed through the melanin, or carbon contained within the former slaves, facilitating movement foreign to those times. The frequencies were so powerful that they put the listeners in sort of a trance, not dissimilar to the Pied Piper of Hanlin, and therefore referred to as ‚the Devil's music'. In fact, even Henry Ford and Thomas Edison publicly spoke out against the blues, ragtime and jazz, saying that they spawned immoral behavior. This interpretation was not entirely untrue as many of the West-African and sub-Saharan melodies and rhythms were in fact used to invoke or call upon certain spirits – be they the spirit of healing, fun, sexuality or damnation. This fear was real as through this music, many musicians and laymen found freedom from oppression, as well as freedom of expression.

This freedom manifested itself in many ways. Initially, those such as Henry Ford blamed this new phenomenon on the Jews saying that they wanted to elevate the Black population above whites because they, the Blacks, were easier to control. This belief even sparked a new movement called 'Square Dancing'. Yes, Square Dancing was actually created to offset the 'wild' immoral dancing, drinking and lewd behavior said to have been associated with the Jazz genre. So these men of power actually began a movement among whites of wholesome dancing with old-time country music. As a result of this movement many states actually adopted Square Dancing as their official State Dance. The kicker is that this type of dancing was copied from the slaves. Ironically, the music and dance used to counter the music and dance of Black people was originated by Black people.

Thankfully, Jazz has survived throughout the ages, taking on the characteristics of whatever style and rhythm happened to rule the day.

Recording

Brown or African American musicians began making recordings during the 1920's as blues and jazz were copied by others which helped spawn a new culture which included the ‚Flappers‘ known for their outlandish behavior. This behavior was attributed to the polyrhythms of ragtime, jazz and the jerky pulse of the blues. Bands were formed using available instruments one of which was the new and interesting Saxophone. Talk about your pied pipers!

To wit, jazz and ragtime also ushered in another African American art form, tap-dancing. According to

Ray Lynch, world renown tap dancer, tap dancing was used by the slaves as a form of non-violent competition because they weren't allowed to fight. It was also the music for the ‚Roaring 20's' which was the platform from which the 'Flappers' sprang.

In a society that barely allowed women to speak in public, the Flapper was an unwelcome irritant. These previously demure white women smoked, associated with marijuana and opioids, openly talked about sex and listened to jazz and the blues. They were known for their short skirts, bobbed haircuts and for dancing like the ‚darkies'. Pioneers of a new era, these women paved the way for women's lib, fueled by the music that drove them and revealed their empowerment.

<u>The Sincerest Form of Flattery</u>

These phenomena influenced many white musicians as well, who became famous copying black artists. The genre was so successful, many white artists resorted to playing jazz music and creating jazz ensembles. None more popular and as successful as Paul Whiteman dubbed the ‚King of Jazz' as a result of his establishing several dance bands that played as or, of big band jazz. To his credit, he did want to use black musicians but was cautioned against it by his agents and comrades as racial tension was a continuing issue. He did however, use many compositions penned by black composers.

They would also use black-face, a satirical homage to black artists as a form of validation of talent, created by painting their faces with black shoe polish. Some of the more famous of this fad included W. C. Fields and Al Jolson.

Swing That Thing

Jazz morphed into 'Swing Jazz' in the 1930's which fueled the big band, dance model. Those influenced by this jazz variation include Jimmy and Tommy Dorsey, Benny Goodman, Glenn Miller and Artie Shaw. I'm not saying that they were bad guys or terrible musicians. On the contrary, these were gifted, music-savvy performers in their own rights. My statement has to do with the fact that black musicians laid the groundwork, or the blueprint for the new genre and were limited in reaping the rewards of establishing such a successful product. These rewards encompass TV appearances, elegant high-paying venues, a multicultural fan base and lucrative record contracts.

Rhythm & Blues and Soul

The 1940's saw a new genre emerging from the combination of swing and blues called Rhythm and Blues. This was cadence-driven, lyric heavy music with stories about relationships and struggles – usually from an urban perspective. The formerly folk driven 'Country and Western Music' suddenly became more pop and began to present life from a rural perspective. This evolved into a musical style that would become known as 'Soul Music', a direct descendant of gospel as the singer used the body to push out the sounds that told their stories. Unlike crooners such as Dean Martin and the like, who based their success on being balladeers, this music was gritty storytelling in the tradition of the village storyteller. It replaced the smooth, mellow tones with emotional outbursts of pure music. This style of music influenced and was copied by singers like Janice Joplin, The Rolling Stones, and far too many other rock bands to be mentioned here.

Country Music

Country music from the 1930's, much like the blues, featured songs of emotional strength and struggle. Backed by simple chords and melodies, it made an immediate and long-lasting impression on America and the world. One of the most prominent characteristics of this genre was the banjo. The banjo is credited to Western Africa and remains a mainstay of one of America's most loved home-grown styles of music.

Boogie-Woogie and Rock & Roll

Little Richard and Chuck Berry were responsible for yet another style of music – forever known as 'Rock and Roll'. This, the combination of boogie-woogie and soul music was guitar driven and patterned after a style created by Chuck Berry and emulated by such singers as Jerry Lee Lewis, Elvis Presley and others who tried to capture this ‚black fire'. It also molded many British bands as well as other bands around the world, captivated by that black sound. It is still one of the most popular styles of music in Britain today.

Throughout the 60's and 70's, Soul Music dominated

the airwaves becoming the music of choice for consumers - so much so that singers and musicians from all cultures, even behind the Iron Curtain had to adopt the style. The fact that the music evolved into other forms doesn't diminish the source in any way, as the metamorphosis of the genre still possessed the qualities and attributes of the original. To their credit, the Beatles and Rolling Stones credit much of their success to the black blues artists of the time.

The songs and melodies are individualized through interpretation or improvisation, thus taking on the character of the person playing or singing. In this time Punk, Funk, Hip Hop and House Music

Punk

Punk Music was led by blacks like Bad Brains or Death with Proto-Punk who pioneered this culture in 1973. Also included in this genre is Hard Core. This united rebels in America and UK racially and politically.

Now, let's throw the combination of Bebop and Soul music, mixed with African and South American rhythms to get Funk. Funk was the expression of soulful lyrics and melodies over driving, syncopated rhythms introduced and made popular by Sylvester ‚Sly' Stone. This spawned a whole new herky-jerky flavor that emphasized and personified cool. The polyrhythms of 'Funk Music' translated perfectly to the new jazz-rock fusion from composers and performers like George Duke, Lenny White, Stanley

Clark and The Brothers Johnson. It influenced white artists like Geno Vanelli, Jean Luc Ponty, Tower of Power and The Brecker Brothers.

House Music, Hip Hop and Techno from the end of the 20th century must also be attributed to black artists. Francis Nicholls or ‚Frankie Knuckles‘ as he was known was from Chicago and is considered the ‚Godfather of House Music‘. His Grammy Award winning remixes in the 80's set the stage for all house music the world over. Then Germans perfected the style and married it with their folk music, creating ‚Schlager Muzik‘ or music with a beat, which is still relevant today.

The 70's and 80's also saw the fusion of Jazz, Funk and Rhythm and Blues or R&B, which became Hip Hop. Hip Hop was introduced in the Bronx by disk Jockeys or 'DJ's', so named because of their ability to play, or 'ride' songs from records, or albums in sequence, enabling people to dance to a non-stop rhythm. In music, there are transitions, normally indicated or initiated by a drum break called ‚break beats‘. These break beats became the foundation for what we now call Hip Hop. A Jamaican MC, or master of ceremonies (so called because he or she initiated the call-and-response that ignited the party-goers), by the name of DJ Cool Herc, who would rhyme during the break-beats. This became the basis for Rap when people began to copy his style. Instead of singing over this evolution of R&B, like DJ Cool Herc, men began to recite poetry that echoed their daily existence. Sometimes that existence was upward mobility.

Sometimes it was the realization of having no options, and therefore, no hope. Oftentimes it was the acknowledgment of rivals and/or competitive social groups or gangs. Whatever the reason for the soliloquies, it ushered in a new culture. Rapper African Bambada is noted for having coined the phrase ‚Hip Hop Culture' and for bringing rap to the mainstream. Rap is the voice of both a generation and a culture that began much earlier than the 70's and 80's. Even as late as the 60's, underground group The Last Poets used prose and poetry to tell of the Black Condition and the system within which they found themselves. So, for this music, which was based on grooves and repetition, Rap was the perfect addition, as the constant pulse or melodies didn't interfere with the messages, but drove them. The normal cry of the Rap culture was "We're mad as hell, and we're not gonna take it any more!"

Rap's infusion into the mainstream can be attributed to Run DMC who was the first Rap group to sell 500,000 copies. Their success spawned the next popular rapper Vanilla Ice, a white rapper clad in red, white and blue.

The culture Rap created is strong and far-reaching as it came with a rebellious attitude and posture, and a style of dress all its own. For example, the plaid lumberjack shirts were a significant statement of social status as they were initially distributed by an organization called The Charity Newsies. Lower income families were given these clothing, along with pants and sometimes shoes and jackets or coats to augment or offset not being allowed to purchase clothing with food stamps. This then became an identity for those in impoverished areas who, in many cases, formed cliques, or gangs, identifying themselves through colors. The oversized pants were also a product of this culture because many of the clothes were just too big. This style and attitude developed into its own culture which was adopted all around the world, and in many places, still exists today.

The rappers that made Rap the voice of a nation includes 'NWA', 'Public Enemy', 'Tupac' and 'Nas'. Though there exist many Rap 'products' in the marketplace, there are some rappers who still embody Rap's initial purpose of informing and educating the masses. These include 'Common', 'Him the Heem' and 'Chance the Rapper'.

Enter the modern R&B Boy Bands like Blackstreet, Boys II Men, New Edition and BBD. These groups sang and performed their songs over the latest genre created by Teddy Riley, 'New Jack Swing'. These high-powered beats set the stage for exciting performances and vocal arrangements. With elements of Jazz, Hip Hop and old school R&B, New Jack Swing bridged the gap between Hip Hop, House and Dance. Of course, the businessmen saw the opportunities to bring this captivating style to a broader audience by creating white boy bands like The Backstreet Boys and N-Sync, to major success.

Michael Jackson Re-defines Pop Music

Modern Pop music would not be what it is today if not for the influence of at least three individuals: Michael Jackson, Prince and Lionel Richie. This genre is called

Pop music because it is popular with the masses, transcending race and culture. Female artists who fit the category include crossover artists Tina Turner, Mariah Carey, the late Whitney Houston and later in her career, the late, great Aretha Franklin. This crossing over is not more evident than Michael Jackson's 'Thriller' album, which has sold more than 30 million copies. Michael Jackson is credited for bridging the color gap, creating and retaining fans of all races and becoming one of the world's first black international icons. This opened the door for all other black inspired genres of music as well.

Here are some of the other black icons who are, and will remain relevant throughout time. These include, but certainly are not limited to: Nat King Cole, Miles Davis, Ella Fitzgerald, Louis Armstrong, Chuck Berry, Aretha Franklin, Marvin Gaye, Kendrick Lamar and Usher, just to name a few.

Black music has created a new mosaic, permeating most cultures all over the Earth. Today's music is directly influenced by Hip-Hop altering how we classify Pop music now and in the future. This was not more apparent to me than when the Sheikh of Dubai booked internationally known dance group La Bouche for his son's birthday celebration. I was most honored and fortunate to have been a background singer for the group and during a pause, the son comes to me and asks me if we could perform some American Hip-Hop. In fact, the genre of Hip Hop and its adjoining attributes are so powerful that China has forbidden the music in any form from its radio and TV broadcasts.

As, I mentioned before, many of the ‚stars' of the corresponding musical genres were created to offset the popularity of black artists. For example, Al Jolson in blackface mimicked black singers; Elvis Presley imitated Jacky Wilson and Little Richard; Mama Cass Elliott and Janis Joplin – great black blues and gospel singers of the time including Aretha Franklin; The Osmonds were created to address the success of The Jackson 5. There is always the search for that black sound in an acceptable package. Hall and Oates, Celine Dion, Anastasia, Adele, M&M, Vanilla Ice, Kid Rock, Justin Timberlake, Ed Sheeran and Rag-n-Bones Man, all hit the market with a distinctively black sound.

Even though the Black community is filled with racial inequality and surrounded by prejudice, it is the music that ties it to other cultures in the world, as it offers a window into the accomplishments and struggles within these communities. It is one of the threads that tie these communities together.

Let's look at the evolution of the advancement or curtailment of black music and black inspired music, the culture associated with it, and its effect on other lands and cultures. As we previously stated, China has banned all Hip Hop and Hip Hop related culture from its radio and TV. This includes music, beats, hairstyles, dress and language. In Germany, there existed a culture related to Black Music and Black music culture that was reflected in the clothing, speech, music preference and general attitude toward black artists. This was systematically changed by popularizing a new style of music, attaching it to a new style of dress, and associating black stars with major German icons in David Guetta and Cro. The media also did their part in insuring that blacks lost their shine or prestige and cache with the black music created by blacks. However, the masses still wanted to hear that sweet soul sound, so now the emphasis is on German Rap and Deutsche R&B - mostly copies of the American originals. The same is true in Italy where Italian Rap and R&B are making a profound impact on the tweens, teens and older listeners alike. In fact, almost every European country has an R&B and HIP HOP genre – in its own language. That's some pretty strong culture.

A BLACK THREAD

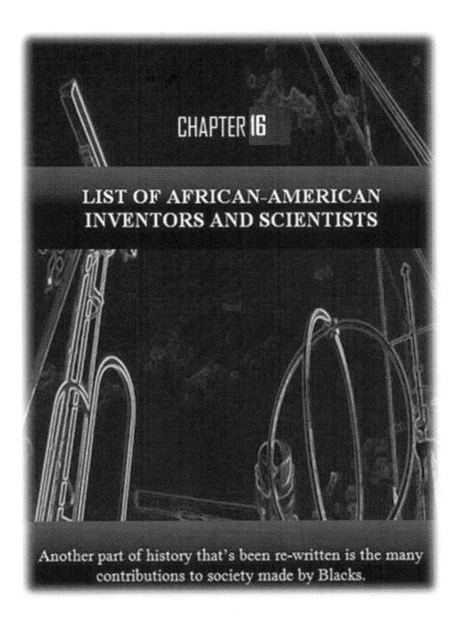

CHAPTER 16

LIST OF AFRICAN-AMERICAN INVENTORS AND SCIENTISTS

Another part of history that's been re-written is the many contributions to society made by Blacks.

16 LOST DATA

The many contributions to society made by Blacks. These show up in the fields of education, science, agriculture, art, music, theater, space exploration, and transportation, as well as other everyday needs. Since the influence of the Moors on modern culture, blacks have contributed to the growth and development of the global landscape in many, many areas. The contributions to literature, science and the betterment of mankind have made life better for billions of people of all nations. Many of these contributions were inexplicably attributed to the handlers or masters of their actual creators. Take for example, the 'Cotton Gin' credited to 'Eli Whitney' was actually invented by his slave. In another famous case, 'Colonel Sander's Kentucky Fried Chicken' supposedly created by Colonel Sanders himself was actually created by his Black servant. For example, here are some little known facts about events and contributions that helped shape the world as we know it today. Below we find some of these inventions and other contributions whose origins have remained hidden from the world for whatever reasons. For example:

- The poetry of Jose Vasconcelos, around 1710, was adopted into Mexican folk-lore so strongly, that his verses helped shape that culture for more than 100 years.

- Abram Petrovich Gannibal was an African brought to Russia as a gift for Peter the Great. He became major-general, military engineer, governor of Reval and nobleman of the Russian Empire. He is perhaps best known today as the great-grandfather of the greatest Russian poet and the father of the Russian literature, Alexander Pushkin, who wrote an unfinished novel about him, Peter the Great's Negro.
- A navigator and explorer of African ancestry, Pedro Alonso Nino traveled with Christopher Columbus' first expedition to the New World in 1492.
- Africans had or invented the wheel more than 7000 years ago.
- In 1862, Mary Louvestre, a freed seamstress and housekeeper helped win the Civil War by copying the plans for the South's iron-clad CSS Virginia war ship. This former slave's heroism actually turned the tide for the Union during this war. She actually had to walk between one and two hundred miles to the north with the plans, sneaking past sleeping Confederate soldiers.
- Bill Bo Jangles now known as a dancer, is noted for having raced a horse backwards, and winning. He was a noted comic whose dancing fame came when he was 50 years old during the Shirley Temple era.
- Dancing was used instead of fighting and used for communication. The cakewalk comes from the masters drinking tea and cake being emulated by the slaves. When the masters saw it, they would

award a piece of cake to the slave who could do the cakewalk in the straightest line.

Black Inventors Who Changed the World

There exists an extensive list of African American scientists and inventors that have advanced society and helped move humanity forward. These include many innovations – from the practical applications of existing materials, to the creation of processes that involve scientific discovery.

One of these scientists was George Washington Carver who was well known for his development of alternative crops for farm families. His thrust was to provide poorer farmers with both food and sources of supplemental income. Of these crops, two of the best known are peanuts and soybeans. To find out more about these, do the research.

He also gave Henry Ford the idea for mass production from looking at the exponential growth of the Fibonacci sequence in plants. To be clear, Ford is not noted for inventing the automobile, his claim to fame is mass production. In fact, Ford's competition included the Paterson Car Company, a Black-owned manufacturer located in Greenfield, Ohio, whose original focus was building carriages. Upon the founder, Charles Patterson's death in 1910, his son

Frederick converted the carriage business to an automobile manufacturer, creating the Patterson-Greenfield car. This car was said to have been better built and more sophisticated than Ford's car, but George Washington Carver's 'mass production' system won the day. The Patterson Company went on to supply the major auto manufacturers with school bus bodies and the like, which companies such as Ford and General Motors just put on their chassis. The company finally closed its doors in 1939, and few, if any, of the 150 cars they built survived.

Another renowned scientist was celebrated research chemist, Percy Lavon Julian, a pioneer in the chemical synthesis of medicinal drugs from plants. The first to synthesize the natural product physostigmine, he was also a pioneer in the industrial chemical synthesis of human hormones, steroids, progesterone, and testosterone, from plant sterols such as stigmasterol and sitosterol. His work was the foundation for the steroid drug industry's production of cortisone, corticosteroids, and birth control pills.

Still another black scientist who impacted America and the world was Granville T. Woods, one of America's most notable (but ironically least known) inventors. Woods received his first patent in 1884 and over the course of his life would invent fifteen new technologies for electric railways. New York would never have the transit system it now has were it not for

Woods seeing and filling those needs. He succeeded in selling many of his inventions to General Electric, Westinghouse and Bell Telephone Company. Here is a list of his other inventions we use today, or at least, have made today's technology and our mobility possible.

The Overhead Conducting System for Electric Railways the 'Trawler' or 'Trolley' (the system upon which the famed German system is built and operates) - We've seen it all over the world – an electrical apparatus that provides electrical traction to the rail vehicle to which it is connected. Today's term for it is the ''Light Rail'

The Electric Railway Conduit System - This system used conductor rails instead of pulleys and cables, the first of its kind. Along the same lines, a version of the notorious 'third rail' was also invented by Woods. This is the type of system that makes many of the NYC subways possible today.

The Induction Telegraph System - The inability of train conductors and engineers to speak to one another in transit was the source of many an accident. This situation was addressed when communications on moving trains were made possible by Woods' Induction Telegraph System, or 'Telegraphony' enabling people to use the same lines for verbal and Morse Code communication. This was actually an early version of wireless LAN (Local Area Network) as it was used as a multiple wireless cab signal system servicing railways. Also, his 'Synchronous Multiplex Railway Telegraph' allowed messages to be sent to and from trains while they were moving.

Woods' electric rail car speed control system used field shunting instead of resistors to slow down or speed up the transport in question. It was this control of energy that improved the safety of streetcars and similar transport, preventing them from malfunctioning or catching fire.

A true genius, Woods introduced his 'Multiple Distribution Station System' which used the principles of electro-magnetic induction and was light years ahead of its time. This invention was at least 100 years ahead of its time and similar to today's linear induction railroad propulsion systems. Imagine what would have happened if Woods had met and worked with Tesla.

There are many, many more inventions and discoveries that aided mankind and the ensuing generations to come.

- Charles Drew - An outstanding athlete, teacher and director, he also pioneered blood and blood plasma preservation techniques.
- Norbert Rillieux – a chemical engineer, noted for the Multiple-effect evaporator - important in the

growth of the sugar industry. 1846 invented a vacuum pan for sugar refining

- A modern-day inventor, Lonnie George Johnson, an engineer, invented the Super Soaker water gun, the top-selling toy in the United States in 1991 and 1992. To date, Super Soaker sales have totaled close to one billion dollars. Johnson holds over 80 patents, with over 20 more pending, and is also the author of several publications on spacecraft power systems.
- Harold Amos was a microbiologist and the first African American department chair at Harvard Medical School
- Benjamin Bannaker – mathematician, astronomer, surveyor, clockmaker, author and farmer. Made the first clock in America and assisted in survey of the original boundaries of the District of Columbia
- George Edward Alcorn Jr. an American physicist. Invented a method of fabricating an imaging X-ray spectrometer
- Archie Alexander Civil engineer - Responsible for the construction of many roads and bridges, including the Whitehurst Freeway, the Tidal Basin Bridge, and an extension to the Baltimore-Washington Parkway.
- Leonard C. Bailey Inventor   Folding bed
- Alice Ball - Chemist - Extracted chaulmoogra oil for the treatment of Hansen's disease Otherwise known as leprosy.
- Andrew   Beard   -
Farmer, carpenter, blacksmith, railroad
worker, businessman,   inventor   -   Janney

coupler improvements and rotary engine patent dated July 5, 1892
- Henry Blair was the second Black inventor to have been issued a patent. Famed to have invented the seed planter and cotton planter
- Kwabena Boahen: Bioengineer who invented the Silicon Retina which is able to process images in the same manner as a living retina
- Otis Boykin: an engineer and inventor. Inventor of the Artificial heart pacemaker control unit
- Thomas C. Cannon - Inventor who led a group of engineers responsible for developing the Tactical Optical Fiber Connector (TOFC), and the ST Connector that helped make fiber optic communications affordable.
- Charles W. Chappelle - Electrician, construction, international businessman, and aviation pioneer. Designed long-distance flight airplane; the only African-American to invent and display the airplane at the 1911 First Industrial Air Show held in conjunction with the Auto Show at Grand Central Palace in Manhattan in New York City; president of the African Union Company, Inc.
- David Crosthwait - Research engineer of Heating, ventilation, and air conditioning; received some 40 US patents relating to HVAC systems
- Mark Dean - Computer scientist Led teams that developed the ISA bus, and the first one-gigahertz computer processor chip.
- Clarence 'Skip' Ellis - Computer scientist First African American with a Ph. D in computer science; software inventor including OfficeTalk at Xerox PARC.

- Sylvester James Gates - Theoretical physicist Work on supersymmetry, supergravity, and superstring theory
- Frederick M. Jones - Invented refrigerated truck systems
- Jim Beckworth opened the pass through the Sierra Nevada mountains
- John Baptist DeSalve Discovered Chicago
- Matthew Henson was the first man to visit the North Pole.
- Jan Ernst Matzeliger Matzeliger successfully invented an automated shoemaking machine that quickly attached the top of the shoe to the sole. This process called "lasting", could produce more than 10 times what humans could create in a day. This invention revolutionized the shoemaking industry and made shoes affordable to the average person. Matzeliger's first shoemaking machine model was made out of cigar boxes, elastic, and wire.
- Lewis Latimer - Inventor, draftsman, expert witness Worked as a draftsman for both Alexander Graham Bell and Thomas Edison; became a member of Edison's Pioneers and served as an expert witness in many light bulb litigation lawsuits; said to have invented the water closet.
- Jerry Lawson - Computer engineer who designed Fairchild Channel F, the first programmable ROM cartridge-based video game console.
- Ernest J. Wilkins Jr. - Mathematician, engineer, nuclear scientist Entered the University of Chicago at age 13; Ph.D at 19; worked on the Manhattan Project; wrote over

100 scientific papers; helped recruit minorities into the sciences
- Lloyd Albert Quarterman - Manhattan Project, worked with Albert Einstein and Enrico Fermi
- Isaac Johnson - Held patent for improvements to the bicycle frame, specifically so it could be taken apart for compact storage
- Elijah McCoy Invented a version of the automatic lubricator for steam engines,
- Charles Brooks Inventor Street sweeper truck and a type of paper punch

This is just a short list of accomplishments of those who came before us. With just a little bit of research, one can uncover so much more. I invite and challenge you to try.

SUMMARY

SUMMARY

There are actual discrepancies in the primary information one finds on the subjects of race and institutional racism. The events that shaped this world had more than one catalyst, as well as, more than one protagonist. Many of these events were driven by the desire for control and domination while others were the results innovation and necessity.

In summation, the information in this book was intended to enlighten. Its purpose is to open young minds to a history previously hidden from them and fill in the gaps that older generations experienced. It is the result of intensive research and in-depth retrieval of lost data.

As a child growing up in America, undoubtedly the best country on the planet, I was told, and made to believe things that were truths from just one perspective. I learned that Columbus 'discovered' America but not that his quest was a continuation of the Spanish Inquisition as indicated by the cross painted on his sails – the same cross worn by 'Tomas de Torquemada'. I didn't learn that far too many Native Americans were slaughtered in the establishment of this new country with the black powder confiscated from Asia. I wasn't told that "and justice for all" didn't include 'all'. I was led to believe, through thorough programming that the 'Redskin' was the villain, not that they were protecting their families, land, heritage and way of life from being stolen. So, I rooted for the 'Cowboy' because the Indian was

portrayed as a savage who just wanted to attack the poor white settlers, not that the settlers pushed them out. I wasn't told that racism was built into the very truths we hold to be self-evident and that all men were not created equal. I wasn't told that contributors to the establishment of America, as well as to the betterment of this world included people from all walks of life.
I wasn't told that most media outlets exist to further the agendas of the select few. I wasn't told that there are at least three levels of secondary education, which include: schools wherein one learns how to serve; schools wherein one learns to manage; and, schools that teach its students how to reign.

I was told to follow the rules. I wasn't told that in order to have rules, a ruler or rulers must exist. I wasn't told that these rulers are able to change the rules at will. Let's understand that previously a rule was handed down by a ruler and was received by the citizens or subjects based on the 'rulership' (kindness or ferocity), of that ruler. The governing bodies have decided that when one talks about the word rule, the natural progression is toward the word 'law'. The original definition of the word law was:

"a natural process in which a particular event or thing "always" leads to a particular result." The most obvious subject of this definition would be the 'laws of nature' which are defined as: "a generalized statement of natural processes; one of the chief generalizations of science variously conceived as imposed upon nature by the Creator, as representing an intrinsic orderliness of nature or the necessary conformity of phenomena to

reason and understanding, or as the observed regular coincidences of phenomena which are ultimate data for our knowledge" including Physical Law and Scientific Law. (*"A scientific law always applies under the same conditions, and implies that there is a causal relationship involving its elements"*).

In other words, a *'Law'* is something that cannot be changed. It affects all of its parts equally, and has to be accepted as divine.

However, the name 'rule' has been changed to 'law' so as to make it undeniable and unquestionable.
Now the law is defined as: a system of rules that a society or government develops in order to deal with crime, business agreements, and social relationships. One can also use the word law to reference a rule or set of rules for good behavior which is considered right and important by the majority of people for moral, religious, or emotional reasons".

Why is this important? It is important because the law governs different citizens differently. A physical or scientific law governs all, or the majority of the like elements it affects, equally.
My issue with this is that the laws are meted out with imbalance. There are a select few who are literally above the law, as is clearly evidenced by those fortunate enough to possess diplomatic immunity, which means that they are not bound by the laws of individual lands. That means that laws are subjective at best, based on where one falls in the hierarchy.
Many of the aforementioned atrocities against black or

poor people here were deemed legal and therefore allowed to have occurred.

I understand the need for government and governing without which, there would be anarchy and chaos. It would be lovely if all citizens would be governed equally. But, that is what I meant in large part with access and privilege.

I'm not perfect and this is not to illuminate the imperfections in others. The only thing I want to accomplish with this book is education. It is a light shown on what was previously kept in the darkness.

To future generations:

Keep the oral traditions alive – *tell* your story. But,

WRITE IT DOWN!

Write your stories. Write down your experiences and what you see. And READ! *"The written word is a primary roadmap to the destruction, as well as the construction of the mind."* - which in turn, also governs the body.

Thank you for reading.

ABOUT THE AUTHOR

JIMMI LOVE is an entrepreneur from USA. Born into poverty, he has become the poster child for 'Yes I Can'! He is a unique talent and a veteran of the stage. A business English teacher, he has won academic scholarships as well as other awards and, on many occasions, has been a key player in the making of history. He continues to reinvent himself—abiding by the ever-changing trends, while maintaining artistic integrity.

His tenure as a grass roots politician yielded major results as well. As a community developer and lobbyist, he helped to bring millions of dollars into a desolate neighborhood, resulting in the construction of 50 homes as well as the reconstruction of 400 + dwellings. He also helped create training programs designed to educate the indigent poor.

A true orator, he is also a dynamic speaker and presenter. Most recently, he founded a German gospel choir, whose unprecedented work has helped and supported thousands to date. The normal reaction to resource deficiency is limited or non-existent productivity. Don't be restricted by your environment - work with what you have.

If you cannot do what you want – then you must do what you can."

Made in the USA
Middletown, DE
28 October 2022